# From Me, To You

## A TRUE STORY

BRIAN GREENLEY

AND

ALISON HITCHCOCK

BRIAN GREENLEY & ALISON HITCHCOCK

FROM ME, TO YOU

*For Olive and for Colin*

BRIAN GREENLEY & ALISON HITCHCOCK

# Introduction

When we feel awkward, we say dumb things, don't we? Well, I do - this book is proof. In the summer of 2010, in a pub in Covent Garden, Brian Greenley, a man I barely knew, told me he had just been diagnosed with cancer. For reasons I still can't fathom, I offered to write letters to cheer him up. Brian was rather non-plussed by the offer; I was no writer and what he needed was a cure not a letter.

Brian and I had met six months previously on a yoga holiday in India. I'd gone to seek refuge from a City job which was killing me and Brian, as far as I could tell, didn't seem to know why he was there. He found me aloof; I found him flaky. I was living in London, in my late thirties, on the hunt for a husband; Brian was happily partnered with Neil, in his fifties, living in the home counties. The only thing we agreed we had in common was that we had nothing in common. Or we didn't, right up until we were in headstand in our final class, when we both farted and crashed to our mats in uncontrollable laughter. A sense of humour (and issues with Indian curry) was what, we discovered, we had in common.

Over the next three years, that offer of a letter turned into over 100 letters I wrote to Brian throughout his treatment. The letters, he told me, accompanied him to chemo sessions, distracted him from his reality and connected him back to a world he hoped he would, one day, be able to live in again. But the letters didn't just benefit him. My impulsive gesture, and Brian's response to it, created the most unlikely of friendships and it turned out Brian wasn't the only one to be saved by a letter.

In 2017, after our story was broadcast on BBC radio, Brian and I set up the charity, From Me to You, to inspire and encourage others to stay connected with friends, family and even strangers, who find themselves isolated and lonely by their cancer diagnosis, because we discovered I wasn't the only one who felt awkward when told of a friend's diagnosis.

During his treatment, Brian kept a diary, only ever intended for his eyes. It wasn't the way he wanted friends and relatives to see him but it was the truth behind the way cancer makes you live. Extracts from those diaries, and my letters, make up this book. The letters were usually written on a lap top, always with a glass of wine at my side, and then printed onto home-made comedy-headed notepaper. And while sometimes it may seem like I'm making up stories, it's actually all true.

Cancer is an illness which makes us feel vulnerable - it is unpredictable, has little regard for the others in our lives and kills indiscriminately. And so, when someone we know is diagnosed, we often feel awkward; it is often easier to look away. Over 30% of people living with cancer feel isolated and of those, 25% go on to suffer from depression*. However, looking away, disconnecting, being afraid of saying the wrong thing, and so saying nothing, should not be options. This book is not your usual grim cancer story of suffering and loss but one which gives hope, shows a way to connect and, I hope, makes you laugh, even if only at the comedy-headed notepaper.

Alison

*Macmillan Report: Facing the Fight Alone (2013)

# Prologue

(Skype Messaging)

Sis: What you doing?

Me: Trying to write that letter.

Sis: What?! To that bloke who's got cancer. What's his name again?

Me: Brian.

Sis: Can't believe you're actually doing it. You're weird.

Me: I know. Should have just told him to drink green juice or meditate or something and then I'd have done my bit.

Sis: So how's it going?

Me: So far... Dear Brian. That's it. What do you say to a man you hardly know who's got cancer?

Sis: Dunno. Try to cheer him up, I guess? Make him laugh?

Me: But cancer's not funny.

Sis: I know.

# CHAPTER ONE

## TELL ME THAT AGAIN, DOCTOR?

**28 May 2010**

What a peculiar day it has been.

Warm enough to sit outside, so I said yes to my sister, niece and Neil's mum coming over for a cup of tea. That's why they are all sitting in the garden now, being supportive and concerned, while I'm in here writing.

Wonder whether we will be able to go on my birthday trip to Edinburgh? What about the sailing holiday to Croatia? Am I being shallow?

Was it only this morning we were in that small room with the woman I'd never met before? I can't remember a thing she said, other than telling me she was sorry and I have Stage 3 bowel cancer.

**1 June 2010 – Barnes**

A new experience today. I've been in a bird-hide. I found it very comforting, almost womb-like. I went because it was out of the house. Kept me busy. I tried to pay attention to the birds but my mind wandered. At least there we had to be quiet, so no talking 'what if's' with Neil. There was some peace being immersed in nature and away from everyone. Maybe I could move in.

**3 June 2010**

I've always understood cancer is serious but never really known anything about it other than people die of it.

**4 June 2010**

I've done some research. As Neil suggested, I've kept away from Google and instead went to Waterstones. I bought a book called Anti Cancer – A New Way Of Life by Dr David Servan Schreiber. I was dying (did I just write that?) to read it but I waited until I got home. I didn't think it was the right material for the 5.35 commuter train from Waterloo.

**7 June 2010**

Most common responses to my news:
'I'm sorry.'
'Let me know if I can do anything.'
'If you have to go for tests, I can take you.'

I don't know how I'm supposed to react once I've told people. I don't want them to do anything. I don't want them to be sorry. I don't want my life to change. I'm not ill. I'm fine. I'm very fine.

**8 June 2010**

I am revamping my diet. Out goes red meat, dairy and sugar. According to Dr Schreiber, these are the devil's foods. Wonder if it's too late to change? At least I can control this part of my life.

I've ordered an organic veg box. And I've bought pomegranate juice. It's supposed to be good for me. A beautiful dark purple. And a pretty bottle. Tastes OK, too. It should do – cost enough.

### 15 June 2010 – London

Met Dennis for a pre-birthday drink in one of those concrete piazzas built for office workers and sandwich eating. We ordered a bottle of red and chatted. I didn't really want the wine as it goes against my new regime, but I drank it out of old habits and not wanting to offend. I don't want my friendships to change. The wine helps with gossip. And laughing – Dennis always makes me laugh. But I already sense there is a shift. I refused a top up. Dennis pushed it and said, 'Come on, you already have cancer. What's the worst that can happen?'

### 22 June 2010 – London

Met the yoga gang for a drink after work. I wasn't sure I should tell them my news. I didn't want to spoil the evening. But cancer seems to have taken up permanent residence in my head – waiting to catch me out, trying to make me mention its name. But they didn't need to know. I don't see them that often.

Suddenly I told them – and I immediately put us all in a different place. I don't think they knew what they were expected to do. Sarah said she's heard reiki can work wonders and Alison suggested writing to me to cheer me up. Who writes letters these days? And, as far as I know, she's not a writer. And I only live in Sunningdale – not a long way from her. Odd.

**6 July 2010**

I have date for start of radiotherapy treatment – 26th July.

I am relieved we are getting on with it, but at the same time daunted. I looked up side effects on the Macmillan website and it all sounds a bit hard core: nausea, fatigue, burning sensations, hair loss, skin irritations and losing control of bowels. Nice.

**17 July 2010**

Told Neil I will be going to radiotherapy treatments alone. There's only so far we need to take the 'in sickness and in health' thing. I don't need anyone to take me or wait with me. I am not disabled. I am fine. I know people mean well but I don't need it.

**18 July 2010**

Dear Brian

I have thought of you a lot since your diagnosis, so here I am, as promised, writing a letter to cheer you up. I have added another layer of complexity to my summer communications – all to be written on comedy headed note paper. Here's the first. Obviously I'm starting the comedy level quite low in order to manage your expectations. I don't want to peak too soon.

Apologies if I don't write very much in this first letter but apparently I have a chronic iron deficiency. I blame it on my recent conversion to vegetarianism of which I knew no good would come. I'm told my iron levels are so low, I wouldn't even make an iron-filing. So, I'm now up to my eyeballs in spinach and watercress and suggest you do the same as you're going to need all the iron you can get for your radiotherapy treatments.

I am actually writing this letter in the Cotswolds. My friend lives in an idyllic, converted barn. She's an artist, so as I write (in between surfing the internet looking for inspiration for my next big career), she stands at her easel and paints. We drink wine, imagine wonderful lives for ourselves, and go to bed drunk as skunks. I plan to stay here for the rest of my life, or at least till her mad German boyfriend returns and throws me out. At that point I will return to Chiswick and find a proper job. Maybe. Someone was delivering flyers the other day and I thought that could be a nice job – no commute, flexible hours, no office politics. You can imagine how that news would be received in the City: 'Ex high-flying

8

exec reduced to flyer distribution as career-change goes wrong.'

Alternatively, I am toying with the idea – on the back of my yoga teacher-training course – to set up classes in the North, near my sister. Or I was, till I discovered they only charge £5 a lesson. I don't get out of bed for £5 (although I'd get in bed for less than £2.50!).

Last week, in a more serious foray into the job-hunting market, I found myself at a networking lunch at the RAC, invited by an old client. After the City, I'm not imagining my new career will be in the car manufacturing industry but you never can tell.

Preparations took all morning. My corporate wardrobe had to be moth-checked and doused in Chanel No5 to be rid of fust. I didn't bother to try on my old 'knock 'em dead, you power-woman' dress as that was only ever really an option with a good pair of Spanx and a bout of stomach-flattening diarrhoea. Instead, I went for something fitted on the bust, and as the woman in the shop had kindly pointed out, 'forgiving on the stomach and hips'.

Shoes were much easier. Shoes never let you down – whatever happens around your waist, you are eternally slim in a shoe. I picked my best killer heels, winced as I put them on, tripped as I walked down the stairs, considered flats but thought better of it. A friend once confided she'd not been able to work out why she was having such a good day, until she realised she'd been wearing comfy shoes. With the same certainty I knew Samantha Cameron hadn't managed to bag a Prime Minister husband by sporting orthopaedic footwear, I knew that my friend and I could no longer be mates.

I almost bought a copy of the FT for the journey but decided to blag it with a quick skim of the Metro. I read no further than the show-biz pages, distracted by my ongoing desire to have a voice and hair like Adele (even if it is a wig).

The lunch was me and 12 men, and yes, my place was right next to my ex-client - practically on his lap. I'd always suspected he had a soft spot for me (perhaps soft not being quite the right word). As he pushed a glass of champagne into my hand he asked:

'So, Alison, still with the same chap?'

'John, I haven't seen you for months, of course I'm not with the same chap!'

He smiled.

Opposite was Clive, a man in his mid 50s with a ruddy face and voice to match. Clive and I discovered a shared love of Pilates, with Clive taking lessons at the same studio as Wayne Sleep. He proudly told that he had been at Wayne's 50th birthday party and the two of them had danced together. Before I could question this dubious claim, Clive was on to his next story — the recent tragic death of his wife, Susan. I overheard him mention her several times more during the lunch and I left with the overwhelming feeling that this poor chap, so obviously still in love with his dead wife, would spend the rest of his life grieving.

It turned out that dead Susan was more or less the highlight of the lunch — no great job offers, no great networking opportunities and not even an embarrassing lunge from my ex-client. An e-mail from his PA the next day told me I had charmed everyone and Clive had already contacted her to say he was terribly disappointed to hear I was already 'taken' as he'd been very 'taken' with me himself. What happened to tragic Susan? Men!

Speaking of men, I have been on another date with 'my man'. I'm discovering he's incredibly clever, using such words as 'derivation' and 'reciprocity'. While we're in bed.

Despite this we still seem to be in a relationship, even though I have to remind him to arrange each of our next dates. Oh, the joys, confusion and uncertainty of a new relationship — and that's just for him.

I suspect it may all end next week however as we're off to Tanguera at Sadler's Wells. I've put our names down for the free after-show tango lesson. He's mortified and is now using phrases like 'you're joking' and 'fuck off' which, to be honest, are words I'd like him to use in bed.

Anyway, Brian, I must be off – the TV won't watch itself.

Hope you are keeping yourself busy, distracted and positive and that this letter has helped you do at least one of these things.

Much love

Alison

### 19 July 2010 – Royal Berkshire Hospital, Reading

Who knew the Royal Berkshire Hospital was such a fine specimen of Georgian architecture? In contrast, their new cancer clinic is all very modern and tranquil. Inside, I came face to face with my new tribe – sick people. I don't fit in.

When I asked the consultant about the start date for the treatment and our plans for Croatia, he told me to go on the holiday. My tumour has been slowly growing for the last 5 years so waiting a couple more weeks won't change anything.

So we're off to Croatia – sod this cancer malarkey.

**20 July 2010 – Dubrovnik**

Today – War Photography Museum. I have been fortunate to live a life that has not been directly impacted by war or conflict. I have lived an easy life. But the photographs still made me cry.

**24 July 2010**

Returned home to a letter from Alison. I never imagined she'd follow up on her offer. Her stories were funny and made me smile but now I'm faced with the dilemma of whether to write back. If I'd known, I could have sent her a postcard from Croatia. I have nothing of interest to say. Think I'll just text to say thank you.

# CHAPTER TWO

## OF ALL THE STATIONS, I'M TUNED INTO RADIOTHERAPY

**25 July 2010**

Radiotherapy starts tomorrow. I shall be visiting the hospital for a daily zapping for 5 days a week for 5 weeks. They'll direct the high dose zapping directly onto the tumour, guided by the 3 freckles they've tattooed onto the side of my torso, and the tumour will shrink – well, that's the theory. I'm assured that each treatment is short and painless. I've googled the machine. Bigger than I expected. Like a supersize of the hair-drier my mam used to sit under at the hairdressers in the seventies; frustrated that its noise meant she couldn't hear the gossip.

**26 July 2010 – Royal Berkshire Hospital, Reading**

Start of treatment.

Day 1 and I am still in a holiday mood. I even posed outside the radiotherapy unit for a photo.

## FROM ME, TO YOU

**1 August 2010**

My Dear Brian

So how are you doing?

Laughing hilariously, I would imagine, at my latest comedy notepaper. That's me earlier this year on my yoga teacher training course. Wasn't the comedy notepaper one of my finest ideas?

This week I have been thinking about your daily trips to Reading for radiotherapy. I imagine you'll quickly bore of the journey. You could liven things up by making rude words out of number plates. And if that old favourite fails, you could critique the hairstyles of fellow drivers. If you'd like, Brian, I could pop over one day and we could drive to Reading together. Like a road trip. Thelma & Louise. I'm happy to bring a thermos flask and an oversized road map, so we look authentic.

While you're in the radiotherapy seat, my resolution is to get fit. In your text you mentioned you are on a new healthy eat-anything-that's-a-vegetable regime and it's inspired me to make some changes too. Of course, for a long time I've been ahead of the Meat Free Mondays campaign with my Tequila Free Tuesdays but I reckon I need to add some exercise into the mix.

I considered the hardcore stuff, like Zumba and circuits, but anything that requires running on the spot or jumping in the air is a no-no, so instead I'm going for an extreme version of something already familiar – yoga – but with heat. Hot Power Yoga.

The poster said, 'Detoxing & Exercise. Guaranteed to burn Calories & maintain Zen'. I tend to be sceptical of yoga fads but I do know a few hot yoga devotees and they proclaim it to be marvellous.

I now know those people are liars. Hot yoga is hideous. Not just because the exercises are difficult, or even that it's hot, but primarily because it takes place in front of a floor-to-ceiling mirror.

'Before we start,' the teacher instructed, 'please make sure you can see yourself.' I should have left at that point – but no, I stayed. How foolish.

Rather than catch my own reflection, I eyed up the sculptured bodies of the Hot Power Yoga regulars, their neon itsy-bitsy bikini-style outfits glinting in the mirror. Soon I would look like them, I said to myself. Among the line-up was a bleary-eyed woman in baggy T-shirt, too-many-times-washed jogging pants and a face crying out for make-up. Poor cow, I thought, until I realised it was me.

In the heat, the sweat came instantaneously. Just raising my arms brought on a hot flush and pounding heart. As the itsy-bitsy bikini-wearers became more toned, I became more red, soddened and flump-like. After 20 minutes, I could bear it no more and melted onto the floor, a sweaty, dripping pile of clothes and flesh. Not only had this happened in front of the class but it had happened in front of me. I had caught every moment of my pathetic exertions in the mirror. I'd tried to look away but couldn't. Like some rubber-necking driver, I was forced to witness each moment of my own pitiful demise. On the floor I stayed for the rest of the hour-long class, every now and then catching sight of myself and feeling ashamed.

I can't go back. Driven out of an exercise class by a mirror.

However, Brian, despite appearances to the contrary, I'm not a flake, so when I spotted a Power Hoop class advertised in my local women's 'everything in Lycra' shop I decided to give it a go. They have small premises on the main high street – with an exercise space at the back, I assumed. I dressed to impress in newly purchased head-to-toe Lycra and didn't look dissimilar to the woman placing hoops on the shop floor, right in front of the shop window.

Yes, you guessed it, we were about to do a hula-hooping class in full view of the hordes of evening commuters. If I thought the mirror was evil, I was about to discover a new low. I wanted to leave but a neon pink hula hoop had already been thrust into my hand and I'd been instructed to warm up with some 'gentle hip swivelling'. Oh God. In full view of the window. I spent the next hour gyrating and sweating (but mainly bending over) with the hula hoop occasionally round my waist but more often round my ankles.

I can't go back. Driven out of an exercise class by a window.

Later, taking refuge with a non-healthy jumbo-size full-fat double-choc muffin, on the phone to my mum, I told her about my latest foray into my new exercise regime. She surprised me by saying she had just taken up Tai Chi, so knew how I was feeling as she struggles to keep up with the instructor.

'Of course, we don't sweat, or have mirrors or wear Lycra,' she said with slightly too much smugness in her voice. 'It's actually very civilized. We exercise for half an hour, have a break for a coffee and a biscuit, and then finish the class. Some of the ladies can see the energy between their hands. I can't. But I do get pins and needles in my fingers by the end, so I think it's doing something.'

So that's where I've been going wrong. Forget the sweating, forget the mirrors, forget the windows. Turns out it's all about the pins and needles.

I have been thinking of you this week on your new regime of daily treatments but I'm not going to dwell on them, especially since you told me they'd tattooed you with freckles so they know where to 'zap' you. Hardly hardcore is it, Bri, let's be honest. I had hoped for something more drastic.

Must go now. All my love

Alison

**4 August 2010**

So now I have another person offering to take me to radiotherapy. What is it with people wanting to be my cancer companion? I guess it is kind of Alison to write again, and offer to drive me to Reading, but it has caused me to feel guilty for not writing back. I don't want to write back. I really do have nothing of interest to say. To anyone.

### 5 August 2010 – Royal Berkshire Hospital, Reading

There was a long queue today. The radiotherapy whiteboard said it would be an hour's wait. One of the machines was broken. I had time. I only had a meeting with my duvet arranged for the afternoon. It seems so strange this sleeping in the day – 2 hours every afternoon. A side effect apparently. They call it fatigue. I call it wipe out. There's no point fighting it. It's crippling and overwhelming.

Tried to read a book to pass the time, but couldn't. Re-read one of Alison's letters. It did take me away from the awful reality of where I was.

Jeremy Vine was on the radio. Trivial conversations about absurd popular news items. They wouldn't change the station. Apparently, Jeremy's popular.

I tried slowing my breath to stay calm.

An elderly man, in a wheelchair, was being pushed in by a woman. She was ashen, her cardigan buttons done up the wrong way. Will this soon be Neil? I have tried to keep positive and jovial, pretend I am superhuman. I act as if the radiotherapy has no side effects, but it does – for the both of us.

When they called my name (eventually), they gave me 2 gowns. One to be done up the back and one the front. I looked down. I was wearing black shoes and socks.

### 7 August 2010

Made 2 decisions today:

1.  Start a blog to let people know how I am. Save me repeating myself.
2.  Invite Alison to lunch to alleviate guilt of not writing back.

## 9 August 2010

Bought rose tea today. It's good for me apparently. Made a cup when I got home, as a treat. Tasted vile. Threw it away.

## 10 August 2010

I can't get that woman out of my head: the one pushing the wheelchair. Would it be better for Neil if I told him to go now? Bad enough I'm going through this. No need to inflict it on him too.

# CHAPTER THREE

## I'M NOT WRITING BACK

What do you call a deer with no eyes?

No idea!

What do you call a deer with no eyes or legs?

Still no idea!

**10 August 2010**

Dear Brian

I love your new blog. You've become quite the writer, almost on a par with me. We may end up battling for top slot, although I think my fine comedy notepaper will win the day. Today's 'deer joke' is the one I trot out whenever anyone annoyingly asks to be told a joke. Don't you hate those people?

Neil looks a bit of a dish, if I'm right in thinking he's the other man in your blog photo? Younger men generally are dishy, aren't they, because they're younger. I find 'my man' very dishy but only because he's barely out of short trousers. If we were the same age, I'd say he was of average looks and could do with a bit more chin.

I thought of you today as I was strolling around Chelsea Physic Garden with my mum. Have you been there in your capacity as gardener extraordinaire? You would like it – it has lots of plants (unsurprisingly), a pointless audio tour which makes little reference to the foliage but when in the bee garden says things like, 'I like honey. Do you?' and a very wholesome cafe filled with people conversing in Latin, including my mum.

As if reciting all plant names in Latin wasn't enough, our racy day continued back at home. From the sitting room, my mum called, 'Quick, quick! Come and see what's going on in your street. It's all happening.' An AA man taking away a broken-down mini was what was 'happening'. Oh, it's all a whirl-wind of life in West London.

Speaking of racy happenings, 'my man' is today racing up a mountain in a 150km uphill cycling slog for a cancer charity. (I'm only calling him 'my man' to you, Bri; in other circles I'm far too cool and aloof for all that sort of attachment nonsense.) Things seem to be progressing – I have been round to his house on two occasions and he has removed his wedding photos from the window ledge. None of his friends know about me, although I found out from his best friend (by stealth and cunning) that he only told his family two weeks ago that he's getting divorced. We never talk about his divorce; we just chat like chums and shag like rabbits. I guess it will all work out one way or another and I should just enjoy the ride, keeping the control freak firmly tucked away in a tightly concealed box.

Brian, are you buying lovely flowers every week? If you're not, you should be. They will make you feel nice in moments of darkness.

I have to go now as my mum says it's time we were off out again as Westfield Shopping Centre is calling her. Have not yet worked out what my charitable pay-back is for all this mother-hosting, but maybe I'll find it in Westfield's Prada store.

Looking forward to seeing you and meeting Neil on the 15th. What shall I bring? If you're doing lunch, shall I bring dessert? Let me know.

All my love

Alison

P.S. We should still do the road trip – we'll discuss on the 15th. Xxx

**15 August 2010**

Very jolly lunch with Alison and the neighbours. They asked her about her letters but she was quite guarded, like when I first met her in India. Interesting that she's not like that when she writes. I had invited 'her man' but he's still recovering from his bike ride apparently.

As she left, I mentioned I didn't feel up to writing letters back. She didn't expect replies, she said. I promised to text to let her know future ones had arrived, should she send more. She seemed pleased.

### 17 August 2010 – Royal Berkshire Hospital, Reading

Two hour wait today. I've been given Who's Afraid of Virginia Wolf and Anna Karenina but I can't settle to a book. Well, not these books – need something lighter. Sick of my playlist. The letters work though.

Bought some flowers on the way home. Wonderful deep purple gladioli.

### 19 August 2010 – Royal Berkshire Hospital, Reading

Had hoped there'd be a letter to bring to today's session, but no. I quite enjoy the company of a pen-pal on my shoulder. Keeps me calm in the chaos of the ward.

### 21 August 2010

Neil has cleaned my car, inside and out. He read that a clean car reduces stress.

**26 August 2010**

Dear Brian

How ridiculous to think I was out of inspiration for comedy notepaper. You can't help but smile when you look at Jumbo, can you? I thought he wouldn't look out of place in your garden.

First of all, I must spend a moment to wax lyrical about our lovely lunch. I didn't need to eat again for the rest of the week, which was lucky as I don't possess your cooking skills (or any cooking skills for that matter). You went to so much effort. And how lovely is Neil? Handsome, good company and clearly thinks the world of you. I know you said the cooking took your mind off radiotherapy, but even so, it must have left you quite exhausted.

So, what's been happening in my world? Life is almost back to normal after Mum's visit, although I'm disappointed that she failed to teach me Tai Chi. When she tried, we were both left gazing at our hands, desperate to see the energy, and me not even getting pins and needles.

She did enjoy our trip to Winchester to have lunch with my ex-boyfriend. Of all my ex-boyfriends, Tea Taster is her favourite and the two of them keep in touch. Interestingly, she also keeps in touch with Pilot Pete, her favourite of my sister's ex-boyfriends.

After lunch, Tea Taster's mother joined us. I last saw her three years ago. I've always remembered her as an old lady in her late 60s. This time, she looked more like a 30-year-old, was dressed as a fashionista and, when she spoke, her eyes twinkled like fairy lights.

'You look amazing,' I said.

'I know,' she replied. 'Of course, it's all down to my 47-year-old live-in-lover.'

She met her beau last year when he'd walked by her beach hut. They'd chatted, 'made out', and have been inseparable ever since. I wondered whether my own 72-year-old mum was seeing this as her cue to make a move on 45-year-old Tea Taster but thankfully she didn't. Instead, she just enquired as to whether he had any nice holidays planned.

I rounded off Mum's trip to the south with a visit to the theatre: Educating Rita with Tim Piggott-Smith. She insisted Tim Piggott-Smith

```
was 'the one who does stand-up comedy'. I said
I thought not but she was quite sure, pointing
out she listens to Radio 4 and knows her
comedians. It was only as we left that clarity
dawned.

'Oh, I know who the lead was,' she said. 'Tim
Vine. It was Tim Vine!'

Much love

Alison xx

P.S. Let me know a date for the road trip.
Should we wear headscarves, do you think, and
have the roof down?
```

## 27 August 2010 – Penny Hill Park, Surrey

Celebrated this evening with Gillian – end of radiotherapy. Seemed right to mark the occasion with my best friend but I was less keen on the non-alcoholic cocktails. Gillian declined to partake and was knocking back 100% alcoholic margaritas.

She asked what happens next. I told her the radiotherapy has a month to keep on cooking and shrinking the tumour. Didn't tell her that if it fails, they'll be offering a colostomy bag. I haven't even told Neil that bit yet.

# CHAPTER FOUR

## NOT OFTEN YOU WISH FOR A SMALL ONE

**10 September 2010**

Haven't heard from Tom and Zoe, or Pete since I told them my cancer news. Maybe we were only friends at the pub. People talk about the side effects of cancer but I hadn't expected this to be one of them.

**16 September 2010 – Heathrow**

Off to Chris and Philip's in France. I have nothing to keep me at home. I'm not returning to work and need a change of scene while my tumour cooks. And shrinks. Who knows when I will have the opportunity to be away with friends again? Spent a pointless hour cogitating on whether to tell Alison I will be away as won't be able to text her should a letter arrive. But her letters may have come to an end as my treatment has finished. Don't want her to feel obliged to carry on. Asked Neil what I should do. He reminded me I am only away for just over a week and asked if that was all I had to worry about.

**18 September – France**

I have set myself some goals for while I am here – a mental and a physical one.
Read Anna Karenina.
Swim 100 lengths of the pool every day.

### 25 September 2010 – France

The Saturday market at Les Vans. More pottery purchases. How will I get all this home? Bought 2 salad bowls. I don't need 1, let alone 2. 48 euros on pottery. I must be crazy. That makes 6 bowls I am taking home. Where has this obsession with chunky pottery come from?

Making excellent progress with Anna Karenina.

### 25 September 2010

Glad to be home. Want to get onto the next stage: back to good health.

No letter waiting for me from Alison, so I guess they're done.

### 26 September 2010

Neil ran a half marathon today. This time last year, I was running in the Windsor one. This year I'm the bag carrier.

While he was running, I needed the loo. After radiotherapy when I NEED to go, I NEED to go. I darted into Starbucks. There was a mother and child ahead of me. I waited. Waited. Waited. I clenched my buttocks. I sang a song in my head. I whistled. When the door opened, I almost knocked them over to get in. The relief of making it to the loo was immense. I cried.

# FROM ME, TO YOU

**30 Sept 2010**

Hi Brian

The joy of the joke comedy notepaper has returned. Hurrah. I admit plastic elephants aren't funny to everyone.

I start today with a heart-warming cancer story, because you won't have heard many of those in the last few months! Once we have news of your shrunken tumour, your story will be heart-warming too.

Recently I met a South African man, Shane, who was diagnosed with cancer some time ago. They caught it late and while the doctors were happy for him to have chemo and surgery to remove the tumour on his spine, they also advised him to write a will and put his affairs in order.

Before his chemo began, on a Christian retreat, a priest offered to pray for him.

'We pray, dear Lord,' he said, 'that during his cancer treatment, Shane will not lose one hair on his head.'

Shane was furious. Of all the things the priest could have prayed for. He had been told he would lose all his hair but he cared not a jot. He just wanted to live, and if that was not an option, then to at least have as much time as possible with his family.

Seven years on, four rounds of chemo and surgery later, Shane is fit and well and completely recovered. However, he still likes to tell this story – throughout the whole of the treatment he lost not one strand of hair.

This week is my nephew's fourth birthday. My sister bought him and my niece each a kitten. My nephew chose the name Pussy for his, while my niece opted for Catty. Bless their creative imaginations.

This letter is a bit bitty, I know. I'm just struggling to spin my comedy magic into it. So it may turn out to be a sincere letter rather than a comedy one, which is disappointing as I see my role in your illness as being someone who can make you smile, not someone who comes over all soppy. But the truth is, Brian, I'm under a bit of a cloud. I won't bore you with the details but I am feeling rather sorry for myself. Something's happened and I'm sad and disappointed.

While I've been feeling low, I've thought about you a lot, as you have faced your cloud with such a positive spirit. You must experience all sorts of emotions but to those around you, you appear so strong. My cloud is nowhere near as dark as yours, but if you can do it, then so can I. You really are an inspiration. I'm not used to being miserable and don't deal with it well, but following your example, I'm facing this cloud with calmness. That is all down to you, and for that I'm truly grateful. Thank you, Brian.

I have a vegetarian recipe for you as I know you're all about the veggies now. It's easy and tasty – I once cooked it for my sister and she enjoyed it (usually she can't eat anything I cook).

Am going to sign off now. I've been waiting for my light spirit to return so I can be funny again, but it's not here and I don't want to deprive you of a letter, as I know my written communications are the mainstay of your life.

I go to Spain on Sunday for a week of yoga and to search for my missing humour.

Lots of love

Alison

**30 September 2010 – Heatherwood Hospital, Ascot.**

33

A double scan today – CT and MRI.

Neil waited in the car.

In the scanners I repeated my mantra: shrunken tumour, shrunken tumour, shrunken tumour.

I will not have a bloody colostomy bag.

I'd rather the cancer took me.

# CHAPTER FIVE

## DO THESE BAGS COME IN LEOPARD-SKIN?

**4 Oct 2010**

How can a scan result take this long to come back? Trying to keep busy but am running out of kitchen cupboards to clean and green things to cook. Wish I was on a yoga retreat like Alison. Distracting myself with a downward dog, remembering how we giggled at the back of the class in Goa, farting every time we tried to do a headstand. Hope she's OK. I've never seen behind her veneer of humour before.

**8 October 2010**

Scan scan scan. Results results results. Come on phone – bloody ring.
Not even a letter to distract me. Thought she might have sent a postcard.
Scan scan scan.
Results results results.

**9 October 2010**

Made a pact with myself. If the tumour has shrunk then Neil stays, if it hasn't, he goes.
I won't let him be that woman with the wheelchair.
Won't tell him until the results are in.

**11 October 2010**

Hi Brian

I don't have a cartridge for my printer (well, I do but I bought the wrong one) so you'll have to endure my hand-written communications, I'm afraid. It's also harder to do comedy notepaper without the help of my laptop, so I'll be trying for comedy commentary instead.

But let's start with what is absolutely not funny – Laughter Yoga. We had to endure an hour of it on my retreat in Spain. Even if you and Sarah had been here, rekindling our Indian yoga experience, it still wouldn't have been funny!

The session was run by the chef, a Kiwi bloke, who wouldn't have looked out of place as an Oompa Loompa in a Willy Wonker film (although, of course, on a yoga retreat you're not allowed to have such unkind thoughts so let's just say he was short and orange).

Anyway, back to the Laughter Yoga (or Crock of Shite Yoga as it should be called). The chef-turned-yoga-teacher arrived in a jester's hat. At that point I knew there'd be nothing funny about Laughter Yoga. The session required us to walk around saying 'Ha, ha, ha. Hee hee hee.' Not funny.

It was all made ten times more embarrassing by the fact that, the day before, the Oompa Loompa had tried to hit on me in the olive groves. I'd gone off for one of my daily 'I'm miserable and must be alone' sessions. As I was feeling particularly bad, I'd decided if I could find enough sour, under-ripe olives, I'd attempt an overdose. Before I'd even found a spot for my ingenious suicide attempt, the Oompa Loompa was upon me, talking about love.

As you can imagine, I was in no mood for such chat. Had I known the next day he'd be standing opposite me in a yoga studio, shouting 'Ho ho ho' and trying to tickle me, I'd have told him to fuck off right there and then, but instead I listened to him as he drivelled on about relationships, art and the universe.

'We'll drink wine together and I'll teach you to paint,' he said.

'Would you mind if I just dug a hole and buried myself?' I replied. And there our romance ended.

On my return to the UK, I came across someone else displaying how marvellous it is to be in love. Just when you've lost your relationship, everyone else seems to be flaunting theirs with gay abandon.

Many years ago, I had a fling with an IT man at work. (I know, not my finest hour and apologies to Neil who is an exception to the IT rule.)

Suddenly, out of nowhere, he wrote a very flowery-worded letter about how he had 'issues of which he could not speak' and so couldn't see me anymore. My friends and I giggled about it and assumed his issues were of a closet-gay nature.

A few years later, I bumped into him in Chiswick. He told me he'd recently moved there to be with his partner. It was very clear to me that 'partner' was code for 'gay lover' and everything I'd assumed about his flowery letter was obviously correct. But just the other day, I saw him out and proud on the High Rd, hand in hand with his lover – a stunning, fit, South American beauty – and female.

Clearly the 'issues of which he could not speak' were not of a gay nature at all. It was just that he didn't want to be with me. Why am I so rubbish with men?

Much love

Alison

## 12 October 2010 – Wexham Park Hospital, Slough

The consultant got straight to the point – the tumour has not shrunk.

I knew what was coming next. I'll have to have a permanent stoma and colostomy bag.

No f*ing way. I might as well be dead. Maybe I should call Jeremy Vine and see what his listeners think. I have always had such little confidence about my body. How crap will I feel with plastic bag stuck onto it?

There was no point going any further with the consultation.

'Thank you,' I said. 'But this is not an option. I'm sorry but I have to leave.'

The consultant called later. Said he'd refer me to the hospital in Basingstoke (a centre of excellence apparently) but also said it was unlikely they'd offer anything different.

### 13 October 2010

Not shrunk. Not shrunk. Not shrunk. My head is full of those 2 words. All day, every day.

### 14 October 2010

My pact. For Neil. The tumour hasn't shrunk and now there's a colostomy bag involved. He'll probably be glad to be released from our relationship. How could he still fancy me? I can't have him stay out of pity. But neither do I seem able to tell him to go.

### 15 October 2010 – Richmond Park

Didn't expect the person I unburdened myself to would be Alison. A walk round Richmond Park was my excuse to get out of the house. I didn't really expect her to be free to join me.

And I actually said it – I told her I'd rather die of cancer than have a bag. I can't say that to anyone else. Not Neil, my sister, nor Gillian – they want me to live at any cost. And I can't mention it on my blog where it's all fluffy rainbows and unicorns. I hadn't expected Alison to be such a good listener. No judgement. No all-knowing wisdom. No pleading. Just being there.

I asked about her broken heart. She said we'd talk about it another time. Bought her a coffee and cake instead; cake always helps I think, whatever the situation.


**16 October 2010**

Date has come through for an appointment at Basingstoke. Apparently, their surgery is cutting edge!

**20 October 2010**

Hi Brian

Now, I know what you're thinking – the comedy headed notepaper just isn't funny anymore. Well, this week, think of it as themed notepaper. It shows that everything in life is a cycle, and it doesn't matter where you join the cycle; you are still guaranteed sun, showers, clouds and storms, and if you're lucky in this life, you'll experience them many times over. Other people may join your cycle, and at other times you'll be alone, but the one thing you can be sure of, the cycle never stops.

This week has been about life-affirming lessons.

Today I was interviewed for a place on the Advisory Board of the Special Yoga charity. Every week, Special Yoga treats 450 children, all of whom have special needs ranging from autism to cerebral palsy to attention deficit disorder. It is held together and pushed forward by Jo Manuel, a power-house of a woman, distinctive by her mop of crazy, curly black hair. She has run the charity for five years, taken it to the brink of insolvency, lost her own money into it and secured Samantha Cameron as its patron.

As I prattled on about my corporate experience, Pilates teaching and love of yoga, sounding positively fabulous all round, a couple wheeled in a young, disabled child. Jo's attention immediately turned to the youngster, whose parents used the centre at meal times (feeding him with a plastic syringe filled with liquid and poured into his mouth). Unable to speak or move, he had somehow managed to communicate that the studio made him feel calm.

Watching this scene gave me a real sense of my own inadequacy.

How do he and his parents get through each day? But of course, they do; they have no choice. But we have a choice; our choice is whether or not we can accept whatever life throws at us. And then to choose whether we can accept it – whether we accept it with the same grace and compassion as I just witnessed in this family. That is a choice we all can make.

Life-affirming lesson No 3 of the week.

So what were the other 2, I hear you ask?

The next lesson of the week was a reminder the old sayings are always the most true. The saying I'm particularly referring to is: 'treat 'em mean, keep 'em keen'.

After four days of tactical silence, the bloke I'd met at Sarah's party e-mailed to ask for a date. I e-mailed back to say OK but when the day dawned, I couldn't be arsed, so cancelled. Predictably, date-boy's keen-gene kicked in and he proceeded to bombard me with flattering and persuading texts and e-mails. There he was, the Greater-Spotted Ruffled Male, disarmed by rejection but with enough testosterone coursing through his veins to believe he could save the situation. Such predictable creatures, men.

And my final life-affirming lesson of the week was you, Bri.

At the hairdresser's, reading August's Vanity Fair in an attempt to look stylish (quite a departure from my usual magazine of choice – Heat, Closer, Hello, OK!), I came upon an article by the author and journalist Christopher Hitchens, entitled 'Topic of Cancer'. Naturally, since your illness, I am interested in all things oncology, so I read on.

He wrote very frankly about his recent diagnosis. He said the normal process of denial, rage, depression and eventual bliss of acceptance had passed him by and he was stuck instead with just a great sense of waste.

He discussed the irony of hearing his latest book had hit the best-seller list on the same day he was diagnosed, and the last flight he'd taken as a 'healthy person' had made him a million-miler and entitled him to a lifetime of free upgrades.

He asked the Cosmos 'Why me?' and heard it reply, 'Why not?'

Finally, he reached the point where he resolved to resist as best he could and sought the most advanced advice he could find – to ensure his lifestyle was healthier than it had ever been and to take comfort from the fact he knew that on his side was 'a group of brilliant and selfless physicians plus an astonishing number of prayer groups'. All of this gave him the strength to know he would get through it all in one piece, even if that piece would finally be a different shape to what it had been before.

As I read the article, I started to have some realisation of where your mind has journeyed since you were diagnosed. I have seen you doing all the positive things Christopher Hitchens finally found his way to but, until our conversation in Richmond Park, I had never really contemplated what the darker side has looked like.

That article brought tears to my eyes, not just for the writer but for my dear friend. And that night, for the first time, I said a prayer for you.

My prayer asked not that you be spared the sad and dark stuff, because even you can't get off the cloud and sun cycle, but that you should always be able to find the strength to deal with the happy and the sad, and that I too, like you, should also find such resolve when needed.

Much love to you as always, Bri

Alison

### 22 October 2010 – Wexham Park Hospital, Slough

Today's trip to see the stoma nurse was designed to reassure me that life with a colostomy bag is a life worth living. She sellotaped an empty bag to my stomach and said, 'Go home with it on.'

So I have.

### 23 October 2010

Sister and niece called in. I showed them my collection of bags. They said that they were smaller than they expected. 'That's because they are empty,' I said. Emma sobbed.

**24 October 2010**

Apparently, for the last 3 days, Neil has been walking round with one of the bags taped to his side. He says he's not sure he's getting the full effect, what with it being empty.

No shit!

**25 October 2010**

Hearse went by the house today followed by 6 black limousines.

Someone was loved.

# CHAPTER SIX

## FLYING SOLO

**25 October 2010**

Dear Brian

This will be a very short letter as I'm rushing off to pick up the tickets for Disneyland Paris, a thought that gets more horrendous by the day. Apparently much of France is on strike & I'm hoping this will scupper all plans, that my friend, her five-year-old son and I will all have to stay in her home town of Rotherham instead of cavorting to Disneyland Paris. Oh my God, Rotherham or Disneyland Paris? I'm stuck between a rock and a hard place. The things we'll do to escape our lives.

And while I hold out hope for a strike, you must remember to keep asking the universe to help you – it will, even though sometimes it appears as if it hates us or has at least forgotten us.

I'm reminded of Sivananda Yoga Swamji's response when asked, after a stroke had left him in a wheelchair, how this had happened, with all his healthy living, yoga and faith in the universe. He replied that for all the healthy living, there are some things that will happen in life that are 'in the blue print right from the moment we are born'. Perhaps your cancer was in the blue print and so the universe's role is to help you deal with it.

All my love

Alison

P.S. Sorry for handwritten scrawl – again. Damn printer.

### 26 October 2010 – Heathrow

Found my courage and told Neil I need to do this alone.

Watching Eat Pray Love at the cinema yesterday reminded me how much I love Italy so here I am, on my own, off to Rome where no one knows I have cancer. I have 2 days to lose myself. Only 1 definite on my agenda: a bowl of pasta and a large glass of red wine, while sitting outside a restaurant in a square. I'll know it when I see it.

This could be the last time I board a plane. I shan't travel with more than 1 piece of carry-on luggage.

### 27 October 2010 – Rome

I walked and walked today. I had no plan. I sat in the Pantheon, looking at the sunshine pouring through the dome. I wondered whether this was a sign there is light at the end of the tunnel?

I went in so many churches and lit a candle in most of them and said a prayer in a few. I am not a religious man but this felt like the right thing to do. I need all the help I can get. When did priests get to look so young and attractive?

I found my restaurant in a quiet square. White table cloths. Handsome waiters. A large glass of red wine. A bowl of linguine and sea food. I cried. But it feels good to escape.

**28 October 2010 – Rome**

Bought a postcard to send to Alison. I'd definitely rather be in Rome than Disneyland. Wonder why she agreed to go there? But then, why not?

**29 October 2010**

I looked up Christopher Hitchens' 'Topic of Cancer' article. It's difficult reading but I get it. He has articulated what I feel but can't write down. Being here, on my own, has made me realise I don't want to be dead.

**30 October 2010**

Neil arrived this evening. I was so happy to see him. We had a delicious supper at a candle-lit restaurant, and life felt like it used to – content being with someone I love. I didn't mention the pact. Who do I think I am? Playing God? Neil has been there these last few months and I know he will be there through whatever comes next.

He loves me and I have to give this my best shot, for the both of us. I love him.

Of course, I didn't say any of this to him.

## 29 October 2010

Hi Brian, or should I say 'Ciao Briano'?

Now, before I go into any questions about how Italy was etc., I would first like to draw attention to my new headed notepaper. How fine is this? And how relevant to me, because when do I ever stop going on about how much I love Mickey Mouse?

And, while I'm going on about how wonderful my written communications are, let's just take a moment to note we're back on with the printed word rather than the hand written scrawl. Life can't get much better than this, can it?

So, Italy. How was it? Spiritually uplifting and beautiful? But more importantly, were you able to escape from yourself for a few days and stare at gorgeous men as they strolled by in loafers and finely tailored shirts?

If you didn't manage that sense of escape, let me recommend four days in Disneyland Paris with my friend's five-year-old son, aka The Child of Satan. In instances like this, not only do you not recognise yourself for the duration of the 'holiday', it also gives a whole new perspective on true misery, and you end up giving thanks on an hourly basis that you will never have to return there ever again.

So why was Disneyland Paris such a horror? Surely, I should have been basking in my own kindness – accompanying a single-mother friend with her son on their once-in-a-lifetime trip.

And paying for my own ticket. What wasn't to love?

Well, for a start, my friend's son (who is called Obi, which could be the root of his problems) wasn't to love. A right brat. He had, at the tender age of five, devised – and got his mother to agree to – a Point & Purchase scheme: he pointed at things and she purchased them.

This ranged from 50 cent sweets to €50 Disney toys. Nothing fell outside his remit. As he steamed ahead, searching for his next purchase, his mother with her purse open, I trudged on behind, laden down with toy space rockets, cuddly Donald Ducks and life-sized plastic guns.

When Obi could be tempted out of a shop and asked which ride he'd like to go on, his answer would be, 'How do I know? Idiot.' This was almost always followed by the phrase 'Whatever, foamhead'.

You can imagine how well these choice phrases went down when we got upgraded to Business Class on the way back, with Obi shouting out, 'Shut up, Mummy, you're stupid,' and always ending each outburst with 'Whatever, foamhead'.

However, I can tell you I made his potty-mouth look very tame as I sat in the Mickey Mouse Cafe bent double in pain, Obi having 'accidently' knocked a pot of boiling water over me. My expletives were far superior to 'idiot' and 'foamhead', I can tell you. Of course, the First Aid doctor was not the French Adonis I had hoped for (or felt I deserved), but instead a Fozzie Bear lookalike. Not even in the medical room could I find a silver lining.

Oh, Bri, I could go on with Disneyland Paris stories: queueing for 45 minutes for a 90 second train ride, following Obi around the Alice in Wonderland maze fifty hundred times, sitting through the same Disney cartoon show eight times – but then Obi is five so what did I expect? Foamhead.

Well, what I didn't expect was the airport gun incident...

...yes, sadly my most embarrassing Disney moment was not courtesy of Obi but rather his mother. One of Obi's prized Point & Purchase rewards was his plastic laser gun. So delighted with it was he that he ran round the airport, pointing it and making shooting noises. Of course, when we got to the X-ray machines, the prized gun was confiscated. Oh my God, you'd think they'd just removed one of his limbs. Obi screamed, shouted, cried, and flailed around on the floor. But embarrassingly there was one person shouting more loudly than him – his mother.

'How dare you take my son's toy from him!' she screeched at the scan operator. 'I bought that in your over-priced, surly country and now you're taking it off us. How dare you? How dare you upset my son. Your country is ridiculous. How dare you?'

And on and on she went. I was mortified. How can you have a friend for all these years and not realise she is, at heart, a fish-wife? I wanted the earth to swallow me up.

The next thing I heard was my friend consoling Obi by telling him he could have anything he wanted from the departure lounge shops. The Point & Purchase scheme was back in full swing. Of course, Bri, you've been to Charles de Gaulle airport and so you know they don't sell children's toys. It's all Armani suits and Fendi handbags. I won't even recount the tantrums that followed.

But, it's all over now and I never need go there again. Thank you for allowing me to unburden all this onto you. I'm not sure who else I could have told.

I really can't go on like this, can I? Hiding from a career, a life, a purpose. I need to get on and actually do something with my life, if only to avoid these nightmares!

Lots of love

Alison

**1 November 2010**

Got a call from Fiona, my colorectal nurse, saying the operation is all booked for a week Friday. Whoa! I wasn't expecting that. I told her I am waiting for my appointment with Basingstoke for a second opinion and to give the surgery slot to someone else.

I was with Philip so I asked him, as a GP, what I should do. In his opinion, I need to get the cancer cut out of me as soon as possible and stop procrastinating. For a moment I was floored but actually I'm not procrastinating; I'm just trying to make the best of a bloody bad job, so let them give my slot to someone else and I'll take my chances.

# CHAPTER SEVEN

## IS THAT SCALPEL SHARP ENOUGH, SURGEON?

**5 November 2010**

All change! I am now going to have my operation at Cutting Edge Basingstoke – the UK centre of excellence for bowel cancers such as mine, and otherwise known as the North Hampshire Hospital.

The less invasive surgery they intend to perform means only a temporary stoma and an ileostomy bag for 3 months and then they'll reconnect me. Can't stop smiling.

Neil has been amazing listening to me weighing up the options. Making the decision together.

This means the op will now not be until the end of the month but it is worth the wait.

**12 November 2010**

My 10-hour operation is booked for Friday 26 November. 10 hours!

I am so lucky – this all feels right.

**17 November 2010 – North Hampshire Hospital, Basingstoke**

I hate it when I snort as I laugh. In public. Happened today as I read Alison's Disney letter. Not sure why she didn't come home early. I would have.

Fortunately, the snort happened before my new consultant surgeon, Mr C, walked into the waiting room. He asked if I was all set for the 26th. I have only met him once and he remembered all my details. Reassuring.

**18 November 2010**

I was surprised by the events of this afternoon. An air ambulance landed at the end of our road. What skill to land there.

Couldn't resist the temptation to venture out to see what was happening. There had been a car chase after a police raid on a house. The police caught up with them at the end of our road. Someone had been injured. The news said the man died.

But life carries on for the rest of us.

**19 November 2010**

You really can find everything you need on YouTube. Guided meditation, breathing exercises, music for goats. I give them all a go – anything to stop the pre-operation heart palpitations and nausea.

**21 November 2010**

Hi Brian

So, I've been in Wales this week. Went for an overnight stay with my friend Judith. I was also going to see her psychic friend who had promised she would tell me everything I needed to know about my future and give me guidance on all those things that elude me – finding a new career, finding a new man, finding a use for the oven beyond storage of bottles of champagne – but on the day she was fully booked, which I guess she already knew.

On the drive down, prompted by the Welsh road signs, I was reminded of an ex-boyfriend, Michael – a Welsh boy done good. Even though he'd left the Valleys many years before, he still loved to tell his stories about life there. My favourite was the one about the local mayor, a slightly forgetful man, who came to Michael's father's wake and said, as he stood resting an arm on the coffin, 'Michael, it's a lovely spread you've put on today. But tell me, how's your father keeping these days?'

Judith, the friend I was visiting, recently lost her mother, ('cos she'd died not because Judith had mislaid her) and had a Welsh tale of her own to add to my collection.

Judith's mother, having been ill for some time, had written instructions to her five children as to what was to happen once she was dead. The instructions were as follows:

- No one, other than Judith, was to touch her. Judith (who trained as a nurse 30 years ago but never actually was a nurse) was to lay her out.

- There was to be no funeral. She didn't want extended family travelling all the way to Cardiff just for a few hymns and a glass of sherry.

- She wanted to be cremated in either a wicker coffin or a cardboard box.

- She didn't want to be taken to the crematorium in a hearse but instead in the back of her son's van.

Before she died, the children told her they weren't comfortable with some of her wishes. They were concerned it may not be legal to carry a dead body around in the back of a van. And if, for any reason they got pulled over by the police, they worried how they would explain themselves.

However, come her death, this loving family did indeed carry out every one of their mum's wishes and are now proud to tell their story.

So there ends my day out in Wales, Bri. I drove home the next day not caring I hadn't seen the psychic as it really doesn't matter what path life takes us on – at the end of the day, we all just finish up in a box in a van.

Much love

Alison

P.S. I'd just like to give you my thoughts on hospital visiting. I have assessed your personality (and I know mine) and I can't believe you will want anyone except family, Neil and Gillian to visit. And let's face it, there's no fun for a visitor, sitting on the end of the bed listening to tales of what's happened to the man opposite and celebrating how many times you've been to the toilet.

However, very happy to visit once you're back home when we can have a cup of tea rather than having to sip on your lukewarm Lucozade. Of course, if you do want hospital visitors, I'll be there in a shot, but I don't think you will.

Anyway, I'm off now, Brian. I did print off the
veggie recipe for you but I can't find it. Will
send next time.

**25 November 2010**

Took my first sachet of Picolax last night – looks like Tango. It's to clear out my system. I daren't even fart today. I am feeling surprisingly unstressed. Think I am relieved the day has finally arrived.

**26 November 2010 – North Hampshire Hospital, Basingstoke**

Woken at 6.30am for another dose of the delicious Picolax. Surely there can't be anything left inside me. Thank God they moved me to my own room with an en suite – when I NEEDED to go last night, I NEEDED to go.

The consultant and his team have been in. I was very surprised there were 10 of them. They said everything was going to be OK. How do they know?

I need to pass the time, hence why I'm writing. Reading a book is tricky. I have read Alison's last 2 letters 3 times each. I have played with my new mobile phone and texted friends thanking them for their messages. I'm surprised how alone I feel despite everyone's well wishes.

Alison text to say she had no idea I was Welsh and hoped I wasn't offended by her last letter. Funny, she's never worried about offending me before!

I have spoken with Neil who is positive but I know will be anxious. I wonder what his morning has been like?

> 'Life is luck, actually. It's quite a relief.
>
> You can do your best, and you ought to do your best.
>
> But ultimately you can't control things'
>
> (Logan Mountstuart - Any Human Heart by William Boyd)

## 24 November 2010

Dear Brian

Hope this catches you before you leave for hospital. If not, perhaps Neil will bring it in. Do you like the quote? I know, not very comedy. But it does bring a knowing smile to your face, I think.

So, this week it's subtle-comedy headed notepaper. And fortuitously timed as I don't want to go too big on the comedy and you split your sides laughing. We don't want you losing any more of your bowel than is absolutely necessary, do we?

So, what has been happening in my world?

Well, most of the week was spent basking in the knowledge that my letters bring you such pleasure, and occasionally they are even so fine they 'move and inspire' you.

I can't believe you share them with visiting friends so you have something to talk about rather than cancer.

I re-read your text as if it was some kind of announcement I'd won the Booker Prize.

I fantasised about being the next Carrie Bradshaw – column to book to block-buster movie – all in three weeks.

Unfortunately, such was the extent of my basking, and so far up my own arse was I, I haven't noticed anything going on around me, and consequently have nothing to write about this week.

Much love

Alison

**28 November 2010**

Dear Brian

Not sure what I'm going to write today but I've promised myself I'm going to send you lots of letters (see above – does the comedy never end!) while you're hospitalised, so I apologise if what you get is quantity rather than quality. You can always throw these ones away if they don't inspire you or make you laugh.

Today I thought I'd steal an idea from a popular style of email I received recently. It was a list of questions with corresponding answers, written by the sender. The form is that you then answer the same questions and send on to another friend.

I'm sure you've received one at some time.

I never fill them in nor send them on but I do like to read the answers the sender has given as sometimes you learn things about friends you didn't previously know.

So, Bri, I thought we'd turn this letter into such an exercise. I'll write the questions and my answers and if you like you can reply with yours (or not).

**Q: Favourite place - up a mountain, by the sea, in a city, in a wood?**

A: By the sea.

**Q: Person you love most?**

A: My sister.

**Q: When did you first fall in love?**

A: When I was 21, with an American, and against everyone's better judgement, I married him. We divorced a year later.

**Q: Favourite alcoholic drink?**

A: That's like being asked to choose a favourite child.

**Q: If you could write a letter to anyone from your past, who would it be?**

A: My dad.

**Q: Favourite country?**

A: India.

**Q: Favourite book?**

A: Right now - Any Human Heart.

Q: **Something you've done you'll never do again?**

A: Go to Disneyland Paris.

Q: **Worst holiday?**

A: Close call between Disneyland Paris & going to Mallorca for a week with a boyfriend who'd forgotten to pack his brain.

Q: **Best trait about yourself?**

A: Can be quite witty.

Q: **Worst trait about yourself?**

A: Always think I'm right (which of course I am, but that in itself is irritating for other people).

Q: **Kindest thing anyone ever did for you?**

A: Lovely work friend Vics taking me away from my desk and to a hideaway coffee shop so I could melt-down in private.

Q: **Best decision you've ever made?**

A: To leave work last year. I think.

Q: **When were you most scared?**

A: After I had an accident and damaged my head and started to think I may never fully recover.

Q: **Thing you're most proud of in your life?**

A: Relationship with my sister.

**Q: Best holiday?**

A: Camping in a tent in the Lake District. Hiking in the day and looking up at the stars at night.

**Q: Possession you treasure most?**

A: My grandad's Crown Green Bowling medal he put on a chain for me when I was 11.

**Q: Best present you've ever given someone?**

A: Sending my mum to NY on Concorde for her 60th birthday. (Courtesy of BA staff discounts – there's a reason my sister's ex Pilot Pete was her favourite!)

**Q: Last time you were a bit naughty?**

A: Meeting a boyfriend for a drink wearing only my coat and heels.

**Q: Greatest fear?**

A: Being lonely.

**Q: Greatest pleasure?**

A: Laughing with friends.

**Q: How would you describe the friend who's reading this?**

A: Very special.

There, Bri, just a short letter but all designed to make your hospital stay more bearable. Will write more as the inspiration lands, and if it doesn't, I'll do us another quiz.

Much love

Alison

## 28 November 2010 – North Hampshire Hospital, Basingstoke

Gillian visited today. I wasn't sure I was up for visitors so soon after surgery, even if she is my best friend. She swanned in as glamorous as ever. I knew I must be pale. I won't be looking in the mirror for a while.

She'd brought goodies: magazines and a bottle of Evian water. Can't be drinking that dreaded tap water, she said.

There's a tube going up my nose and into my stomach, draining the bile and stopping the vomiting. I hate being sick. I always cry. Why is that?

She sat on the bed, swinging her legs, pretending not to look at the tube.

I asked her what she thought to my new designer accessory. She said she'd been wondering what it was and then shrieked at the thought it might be permanent.

Thank God it's not – I'd never be able to leave the house.

Neither of us mentioned The Bag.

When the room went quiet, I suggested she turn on the radio. She seemed relieved but a second later I was shouting for her to turn it off. It was bloody Jeremy Vine.

### 30 November 2010 – North Hampshire Hospital, Basingstoke

Fancy Alison having been married – didn't have her down as the impetuous type. And her sister is her favourite person? She hardly gets a mention in the letters.

Probably won't share this letter with Neil – she may not appreciate becoming known as the 'coat and heels' girl! Struggling to get that image out of my mind.

### 29 November 2010

Hi Brian

In my mission to be a prolific convalescence-helping writer, the quality of my letters may be suffering. However, Bri, I am willing to risk my reputation for the sake of your entertainment. What a friend I am.

I have to tell you how brilliant Neil has been, keeping us all informed of how you've been getting on. I had been concerned I may not know how you are but, oh goodness, I needn't have worried. You can barely fart without us all being e-mailed about it or it being included in one of Neil's blogs (maybe farting isn't the best example as I don't imagine there's much of that going on. At least there's one upside to an ileostomy bag).

It's been wonderful to know how you are. I sent a card to tell Neil how amazing he's been. I'm sure he can't imagine behaving any other way, but we all know someone else who would have behaved very differently. What a star he is.

Now, back to me, never forgetting I am essentially shallow.

Let me tell you about going to No 10. You'll have spotted the picture of Dave and Sam waving me off after our meeting.

I'd gone along as chief bag-carrier to Special Yoga charity founder Jo, who had a meeting with Sam Cam to discuss her patronage for a proposed charity art auction. In a fit of wanting to be involved, I'd agreed to join the charity art auction committee. I thought this may be a mistake, what with me knowing nothing about art, but it seems that if it's all about trips to Downing Street I'm ideally suited.

A student protest meant we couldn't enter via Whitehall (scuppering my chance to feel grand), so instead we used the tradesman's entrance at the opposite end of the street – flippin' students. However, my moment of grandeur wasn't totally ruined as I was permitted through the gate while Jo had to wait on the other side until they'd security cleared her. She was then allowed to follow me.

I smiled at the lone photographer opposite No 10 but he didn't bother to lift his lens. I turned on my heels and stepped up to the door.

Once inside, a stooping old man with a smiling face asked our names, ticked us off a list and enquired as to whether we had mobiles. Beside him stood two large cabinets with pigeon holes filled with phones.

'Take a ticket from a hole and put your phone in,' he said, chuckling. 'The ticket is your contract with us. You see, all these phones, you have to have a way to get yours back.' He scratched his head and continued, 'Oh, but on the other hand, why don't you ladies keep yours in your bags? Put the tickets back. We won't tell anyone.' And he winked.

Not for the first time in my life, I wished I better understood my phone. What could I now do in Downing Street that others were being denied? Could I play a recording of Nick Clegg ranting, 'I'm in charge, I'm in charge'? Could I video

# FROM ME, TO YOU

George Osborne sliding down the banister and sell it to You've Been Framed? No, of course I couldn't. I barely knew how to put the phone on silent, let alone do anything else. Instead, I satisfied myself with a selfie as we ascended the famous staircase of portraits, although I was so nervous of being caught with this weapon of mass destruction, I stumbled in my heels and not only missed capturing my face but also any sort of proof I was even in the building. It was then I was struck by how inappropriate my diamante phone cover was for a meeting with the ever-stylish Sam Cam. I shoved it deep into my bag and instead whipped out my notebook – I hadn't felt able to stretch to Smythson, so had instead gone for something Moleskine from WHSmith.

While walking past a room of suits, I heard David Cameron's voice booming out. Wow! I was seeing and hearing the PM in action. Get me. And I had my phone: I could take a pic. Video him.

Suddenly I was struck with fear. My phone ringtone. The phone I had struggled to even put on silent. The ringtone I had thought so funny the other night when I was drunk. The wolf-whistle. The big-burly-builder wolf whistle. Oh my God, if anyone were to call me, I'd be wolf whistling David Cameron. Shit.

I darted away, catching up with Jo and Sam Cam's PA, who was apparently taking us into No 11 – were we going into The Camerons' private apartment? Exciting.

We weren't. We were going into some broom cupboard of a meeting room.

I shoved my bag under the seat, took off my Reiss coat, straightened by Boden jumper (channelling PM-wife at all times), placed the Moleskine on my knee and crossed my ankles and...

Oh my God, my phone. I needed to turn it off or in some way disable it. But Sam Cam's PA was now in full flow and I was required to take notes. I sat, shoulders tensed, imagining how, at any moment, Sam Cam was going to enter the room and be greeted by a coincidentally timed wolf whistle.

Oh God, please don't let it happen, please don't let it happen. Please no one call me. Why hadn't that man at the door done his job properly and taken the phone away?

It turned out Sam Cam was picking up one of her children from dance class so didn't join us. The PA sorted out everything and the meeting was over. And I was so unpopular no one had even phoned.

On the way out, the stooping old man was gone (probably sacked for security breaches) and replaced by a much more serious chap. He asked if we had a phone to collect!

I felt the wolf whistle tension drain away as I stepped out. Hurrah. I'd survived without embarrassment. Thank God. The photographer was still in place. I couldn't help but look over just in case he decided we actually did warrant a shot this time.

And of course, just as I looked over, my stupid phone rang. But even a wolf whistle didn't get him to lift his lens. Miserable git.

And that was it - my visit to No 10 was done. Of course, I didn't get a chance to lobby on behalf of the students or fight the cause of the working classes but I did manage to put a word in for you, Bri, and I'm delighted to hear a private room was secured for you at Basingstoke. May be the Conservatives aren't all bad.

Will away now so I can post this and immediately start writing my next missive. My mission is relentless.

Much love

Alison

**2 December 2010 – North Hampshire Hospital, Basingstoke**

My sides split. They undid a staple and I came pouring out. Thought I was going to die. The room was suddenly full of people. I wanted Neil. I have now been stitched back up.

**3 December 2010 – North Hampshire Hospital, Basingstoke**

Everyone is being super attentive. I feel shit. And now I have a line into my neck that is feeding me.

**6 December 2010 – North Hampshire Hospital, Basingstoke**

Panic. My willy is huge. Swollen. I'm the size of an elephant. Apparently, it will go back to normal when I'm up and about. Shame.

**7 December 2010 – North Hampshire Hospital, Basingstoke**

Today I changed The Bag myself. This time, I couldn't look away as I have been doing whenever the nurses change it. Amy, the lovely stoma nurse, was there as was Neil and 3 medical students – quite an audience.

I leaned over the sink – naked, disfigured, bloated. I slowly removed The Bag and carefully placed it in the waste bin. I saw the stoma for the first time. Some people call it a rosebud, God knows why. Mine looks like an alien. My insides are now stitched onto my outsides.

I gently wiped the alien with a damp cloth, wincing at the sensitivity and fearful of damaging it. I found the process strangely intimate and at the same time an out of body experience. I attached the new bag, making sure the stoma fitted through the hole so the waste can flow in. Amy congratulated me and said, 'You're on your own now.'

**7 December 2010**

Hi Brian

Oh no, Brian, it sounds like you've been having quite a time of it, lulling us all into a false sense of security, claiming to have come through the surgery incident-free (even allowing your press office to release photos of Perky Bri sitting up, smiling for the cameras) only to then shock us all with the news of a second operation and stories of tubes and painkillers galore. I hope you are now well on your way to proper recovery.

While you've been sitting in your hospital bed, Bri, the UK has been battling with the snow.

Well, that's all of the UK except west London. My mum and sister were snowed in, commuters were stranded on trains, but Chiswick has seen nothing. Or at least till this morning when we managed to get one powdery inch.

I overheard this conversation in the local coffee shop.

'Dave was due to come down to see me this week but he literally can't get out of Edinburgh. Snow up to his waist and the airport and rail stations all closed, he says.'

'That's a shame.'

'I know. I suggested he build a snow-woman of me so he wouldn't get lonely, and the cheeky fucker said he couldn't as there wouldn't be enough snow for my tits. I told him we've had an inch of snow here, which would be more than enough to make a snowman of him.'

As if I wasn't cold enough here, I'm off to Munich this weekend, which is apparently even colder and snowier. However, Rosy has promised me a Christmas market and warming mulled wine, so no doubt I'll survive. Will write once I'm back.

Much love, Brian

Alison

P.S. Can you believe it's a year since we met in India, yoga-farting at the back of the class? Who'd have thought we'd still be in touch? Looks like we're stuck with each other now! Well, you're stuck with my letters!

**9 December 2010 – North Hampshire Hospital, Basingstoke**

Some good news. I have won £1,000 on the premium bonds. That's Christmas taken care of and some new baggy tops and trousers to hide The Bag. I'm aiming for the Monty Don casual gardener look.

**10 December 2010 – North Hampshire Hospital, Basingstoke**

The stoma farts. And without notice. Delightful.

**11 December 2010 – North Hampshire Hospital, Basingstoke**

Bag leaked today. The nurse spotted it – poo on my hospital gown. I apologised profusely.

**12 December 2010 – North Hampshire Hospital, Basingstoke**

I've not eaten anything for 2 weeks but I'm the heaviest I've ever weighed. I've told the dietician I'm not impressed.

**13 December 2010 – North Hampshire Hospital, Basingstoke**

I love this dietician. I lost 6kg overnight. I'm now the lightest I've ever been.

**14 December 2010 – North Hampshire Hospital, Basingstoke**

I can go home today. I have more luggage than when I arrived. Books unread, magazines still in their plastic wrappers. I have a huge carrier bag of pills and another of ileostomy bags. A diet list of what I can and cannot eat – no seeds, sweetcorn or popcorn. And I have Alison's letters. They're coming home with me.

**15 December 2010**

I'm home. Feels like Christmas is here already. We've never had the tree up so early. And it snowed last night. I can do this.

# CHAPTER EIGHT

## WALKIES, LOVE AND CRUFTS

**30 December 2010**

Hi Brian

I'm squeezing in a letter between Christmas and New Year as once my India/Dubai holiday kicks in next week you will find yourself in a letter-hiatus (although you may be thankful for the break!).

Things seem to be on the up for you – the Professor Stephen Hawking style texts are no more – *Brian is OK and thanks you for your kind messages* – and we're back to normal Brian texts – *Glad to be home but missing daily bed bath from that rather handsome male nurse (smiley, winky face)*.

Neil continues to be a star with his updates and has all the medical terms down to a tee. I reckon if you need more operations, he could be lead surgeon.

It's that weird time between Christmas and New Year when us singletons feel more single than ever but I've not been wholly forgotten as Tea Taster invited me out for dinner last night. (I hadn't seen him since my trip to Winchester with his cougar mother). What I had forgotten, however, from our previous dating life, was how 'entertaining' he can be.

The restaurant was small, cosy and filled with the buzz of people thankful not to be eating turkey. As soon as we'd walked in, Tea Taster spotted Sticky Toffee Pudding on the specials board.

'Oooh, I'm going to have that,' he said, smiling in anticipation.

But when it came time to order our desserts, the mood somewhat soured.

'I'm sorry sir,' the waiter explained. 'We've sold out of sticky toffee pudding.'

Tea Taster wasn't happy but consoled himself with a crème brûlée with extra clotted cream.

Ten minutes later, two sticky toffee puddings were delivered to the couple at the next table.

'What?' Tea Taster exclaimed. 'They ordered after us. How've they got those? I need to speak to someone.' He swivelled in his chair, huffing and puffing, his hands flailing for attention.

Tea Taster was about to theatrically explode. As he gesticulated to the waiter, spinning around to point at the offending desserts, I was laughing so much I had to explain to the sticky-toffee couple what was happening. They chuckled, the woman even offering to share.

Meanwhile, the waiter continued his apology.

'I'm so sorry, sir. They ordered as soon as they came in.'

Tea Taster shook his head, telling the waiter that it was just not good enough and he'd like to speak to the owner (Rick Stein!).

'Who orders their dessert as soon as they sit down?' he exploded. 'Ridiculous way to behave.'

The waiter looked as if he was about to cry, so I stepped in to explain that my dining companion wasn't being serious; he was just pulling his leg. The waiter looked terribly confused, hindered by the fact English was not his first language, and gratefully retreated into the kitchen – but not before clocking Tea Taster leaning over towards the neighbouring table and spooning himself a huge scoop of the woman's dessert.

'Have some more,' she offered.

'Well, it is delicious,' he said, 'as I imagined it would be. Thank you very much.'

Having paid the bill without incident, we got up to go. Well, I did. Tea Taster tried to get up but his legs tangled around the chair. He lost his balance and went arse over tit. As he went down, he caught the cloth of the neighbouring table, pulling down onto himself two almost empty sticky toffee pudding bowls, with a final mouthful of pudding tipping out onto his shirt.

Realising his opportunity, he pulled his trapped hand from beneath his back to retrieve the final coveted morsel but the waiter was ahead of him, swooping down with napkin in hand to remove the prized food from his chest, dropping it into a clean bowl and presenting it back to the sticky toffee couple with a flourish, a clean spoon and delighted grin.

'Noooooo,' cried Tea Taster from the floor, pointing at the pudding. 'Surely that's mine now.'

The couple laughed. The other diners laughed. And I laughed – so much so that I forgot to offer a hand to him, the upended beetle struggling to right himself.

My attention only came back when one diner called out, 'I'm sorry, mate. We're all laughing at you and we shouldn't 'cos we've all had our sticky toffee pudding and it was bloody delicious.'

As we left the restaurant, Tea Taster, much to his delight, was applauded. Outside, the two of us bent double in uncontrollable laughter, Tea Taster comically cursing the waiter and saying Rick Stein would do well to restrict his menu just to fish in future.

I can't remember the last time I laughed so much, Brian, or so much enjoyed a night out. And as we walked away from the restaurant, Tea Taster took my arm and said, 'I didn't embarrass you this evening, did I?'

And once again we were back to uncontrollable laughter!

Much love

Alison

**1 January 2011**

I have a New Year's resolution – getting a dog. Neil thinks it'll be a responsibility we don't need and we should consider it carefully. I tell him dog walking will be good exercise and I'll have someone in the day when everyone has gone to work and I'm left alone at home with only mindless daytime TV for company (which is very much geared to a female audience I've noticed. I'd write to someone about that if I could be arsed).

But ultimately, if I need to, I shall play the C-card and Neil will shut up. This could be my last chance to have a doggie friend.

## 4 January 2011

Loving my new hobby – researching dogs. It's very handy having dog-loving Ruth as a neighbour. She volunteers at the local rescue centre and is going to keep an eye out. And I feel better getting a rescue dog rather than one from a dealer. Maybe we will rescue each other.

## 5 January 2011

Spent most of today day dreaming about how wonderful it will be to have a dog.

## 10 January 2011 – RSPCA Millbrook, Chobham

Colin is one of the homeless of Slough – no tag, no chip. On our short walk he pulled on the lead and sniffed a lot. We sat on a bench and chatted. Well, I chatted, he listened.

I've reserved him and he'll be with us in a few weeks once they've done all the checks on us. It was love at first sight. That's a first for me.

### 15 January 2011 – RSPCA Millbrook, Chobham

Forgot Neil has a say in getting a dog (in theory) so off we went to the centre for him to meet Colin. I was more nervous than when I introduced Neil to my family.

Only Neil could come up with so many downsides to having a dog. Blah blah blah. White noise. When Colin climbed up onto his lap however, the deal was sealed. Clever dog.

### 7 January 2011

Dear Brian

I write from the plane on my way to India. Am so looking forward to being back where we met even though I know it will seem odd not to have you and Sarah there this time. But yoga reminiscing is for another letter. Today's communication is to tell you about my New Year.

I'd been invited to spend it in Suffolk with my 'four gays on a bus' friends. They acquired this title when I first met them in India five years ago. I was there trying to find myself; it was

10 months after my dad's death and, feeling I'd neither grieved sufficiently nor in a suitably dramatic manner, I'd decided to take myself off to India. After a couple of days in the sumptuous five-star Imperial Hotel in Delhi, I made my way to Pushka – a lakeside town of great religious and spiritual significance, the guidebook told me. If I was to find myself anywhere, surely it would be there. (As it turned out I was nowhere to be seen in the dirt and grime of Pushka. I've since suspected I was actually in the five-star Imperial Hotel the whole time.)

Instead of finding myself, I found John, Jonny, Atholl and Alistair: four friends travelling round Rajistan on a Jules Verne bus. They took me under their wing, invited me to join them, and we've been friends ever since.

And so, this year, I was invited to their New Year bash. The party was in full swing when a couple arrived, introducing themselves as Kate and Peter, each one carrying a Pekinese ball of fur which they claimed to be dogs. As I chatted to Kate, I heard a familiar voice. They must have turned on the TV, I thought; I recognised the voice.

Of course, the TV wasn't on and, instead, the Peter holding the dog was the one and only great Crufts and Blue Peter supremo, Peter Purves. You'll be pleased to hear I was totally cool and didn't shout out, 'Oh God, you're that Peter' but instead just stared at him as I contemplated the fact I was in the presence of Petra's Dad.

Naturally, I placed myself right next to him at dinner.

Here's what I learnt:

> 1) Peter has been asked many times to appear on I'm a Celebrity, Get Me Out of Here but always turned it down, even having been the action man of Blue Peter.

> 2) Despite his 30 years presenting Crufts, Peter knew nothing about dogs until he met his wife. Today he's more of a dog nut than she, and referred to his own Pekinese dogs as, 'my little sweetie puffs'.

> 3) He has most recently been giving talks on cruises. I imagine he fields many questions about whether he ever shagged Valerie, did Petra really live with him and would he ever sell his Blue Peter Gold badge? I didn't ask him any of these questions.

For the rest of the evening, I turned my attention to David, a very charming man with a loud, posh voice. He said he owned an auction house, so I asked whether I'd ever have seen him on the BBC's Cash in the Attic.

'Yes,' he replied. 'Although more often on ITV's Flog It.'

Twice a year he holds royal sales. Anyone connected to the royal households can offer for auction memorabilia they've 'acquired'. David produces a catalogue which the Queen vets. One item she recently asked to be removed from sale was a letter to one of her race-horse trainers. It went something like this:

'Dear Blah blah blah,

I'm so sorry I didn't get to the race last week but you know how I hate the drive down there. Also my second son just arrived back at the palace and I didn't want to leave him there on his own.

However, we watched the race on TV and I was delighted with our win. I was jumping up and down in front of the television as she came in.'

After a thoroughly enjoyable New Year's Eve, I left the following day, the 'four gays on a bus' mincing off to a pantomime in Norwich, where a friend was playing the Fairy Godmother.

They left me with this funny tale.

They are friends with a couple of ladies in Suffolk, Cookie and Margaret. No one's sure if Cookie and Margaret are lovers but at 90 and 85 it doesn't seem important. Just before New Year the two were on their way home from a party,

Cookie, as usual, in the back, Margaret driving. It was around midnight. A few miles into the drive, they were pulled over by the police.

'Have you ladies been drinking?' the policeman asked.

Cookie leaned over the front seat, looked at the policeman and said, 'We've been at a party since 7pm. Of course we've been drinking.'

Much love to you

Alison

**12 January 2011**

I have an oncologist appointment next week and I'm not yet allowed to drive, so I did a dry run on the train with The Bag.

Neil assures me there is no smell but I sat away from other travellers, just in case.

**13 January 2011**

Someone from work called today. Apologised for bothering me but could I remember some detail on an ex-pat client's last tax return? Six months ago I'd have been dealing with it myself. Now I am a million miles away from that life. I said I was sorry I couldn't help. He didn't ask how I was.

## 14 January 2011

Lovely lunch with Gillian. Well, it was lovely in my mouth but I'm learning that doesn't translate to lovely for The Bag. Mashed potato equals bag full to bursting within 2 hours.

## 15 January 2011

Shopping today. Only went to John Lewis so never too far away from a loo. You can rely on John Lewis for a clean and accessible toilet.

I'm kitted out in my Monty Don look: loose-fitting top, baggy trousers, braces. Wearing size extra-large hides a multitude of embarrassments. And once Colin arrives, I shall have even more in common with Monty.

To celebrate my trip out, I had a very small glass of red wine with our roast dinner. Vile. Tasted like metal. Another thing off the food list.

Food list so far:

Avoid: Red wine – metallic tasting

Avoid: Inflating mashed potato

Avoid: Cabbage – at least cancer's good for something

Eat: Roast chicken – good

Eat: Gravy – good

Eat: Yorkshire pudding – surprisingly good

I woke up at 2am with a warm sensation across my tummy. The Bag had leaked. First time since hospital. I went downstairs and sat on my own for an hour. Removed chicken, gravy and Yorkshire pudding from the list.

**17 January 2011**

Neil has suggested I note down things I have achieved since leaving hospital. It will make me feel better he thinks.

1. Been on a train – on my own.
2. Changed The Bag in a motorway service station.
3. Lost any enjoyment alcohol may previously have given.
4. Bought some baggy clothes.
5. Watched Man City beat Wolves 4-3 on TV – this made Neil happy which should, apparently, make me happy.

# CALL ME SHALLOW

**17 January 2011**

Dearest Brian

Am in Dubai, having left India feeling calm, contented and stronger. I would happily have stayed longer but it is nice to be here with its simple pleasures - flushing toilets, mattresses filled with something other than straw, and food which is not curry!

India was as wonderful as ever. Jodi's yoga classes were as beautifully calming as before and while it was a different group of people, everyone was friendly, interesting and better than me at yoga!

We visited the market, just as we did when we were there, and bought the obligatory sarongs, silver trinkets and pirate DVDs. But this time we did not get drunk at the 'secret' alcohol stall and spew out our life stories to one another, so I had no one telling me to find my inner warrior and leave the security of my city job; no one telling me there is more to life than high-flying careers and big salaries; and no one telling me that once you get to a certain age, wrinkle creams just won't cut it. Instead, this time, people told me they envied my stress-free, care-free lifestyle! I guess the view of the church is different from every gravestone. Did someone famous say that or did I just make it up?

Anyway, I guess what I'm saying is there was no equivalent of you there, no one with a listening ear, a wise heart and a sarcastic tongue. It seemed so odd being there without you. Back then, just six months before your diagnosis, cancer was an illness that affected other people and we were just two people who happened to be on the same holiday. How life moves on.

This time I shared a room with a lovely girl. She was quite private and unassuming. After listening to me prattle on about my super non-working life, my volunteering for charity and visits to Downing Street, she revealed she had founded a charity 16 years ago – a super successful media centre housed in a state-of-the-art building made of straw. She had been awarded an honorary doctorate last year. Her yoga practice was also very accomplished. The only way I could top trump her was to remind her she hadn't had the teacher dedicate a reading to her to thank her for her humour, like the teacher had done for me. She agreed she hadn't had this accolade but added that with so many Americans in the group, it wasn't difficult for me to be the funniest person there. Who said yoga wasn't competitive?

The calm of the yoga holiday quickly faded once I boarded the plane to Dubai. Among my fellow passengers were a group of Indian men on their way to the Middle East. On arrival, I'm sure they would have been shipped off to a building site, ferried around in overcrowded buses and accommodated in 100-bed dormitories.

Though while still on Indian soil, they were kings. Decked in cheap jewellery and even cheaper suits, they sat proudly, running fingers through slick-backed hair. They had at least two mobile phones each, chatting on one, texting on the other, and once airborne, they refused to turn them off, instead photographing the cabin and each other. I found it sad that these swaggering men, once landed in Dubai, would be treated as a cheap, labouring commodity, barely of any value to anyone. But maybe that's not how they see themselves. I certainly hope not. I guess everyone's starting point is different; we all have a varying set of values and needs.

But now I must sign off as I need to take advantage of all the luxury shopping, dining and general soullessness that Dubai has to offer. Perhaps here rather than India is my true spiritual home?

Much love

Alison

## 20 January 2011 – King Edward VII Hospital, Windsor

Another hospital, another consultant. This time it's the oncologist, responsible for my treatment plan from now on. Two hour wait to see him. At least there was no bloody Jeremy Vine.

There are cancer cells in one of the lymph nodes, and there's no way of knowing whether more are floating in my blood stream. As a precaution, I'll be having the threatened chemotherapy. This is all quite normal apparently.

I know this is the best course of action. It will obliterate the cancer completely and I'll have some peace of mind.

The consultant recommends I keep The Bag during the treatment, so it looks like my new friend will be hanging around for longer than the 3 months I'd hoped.

# CHAPTER NINE

## THELMA & LOUISE

**1 February 2011**

Start date for chemo: 16th February.

**2 February 2011**

Gillian says she's aware she's not joining me with my healthy eating and drinking regime and doesn't really get all the yoga and alternative stuff, so instead she's been asking round the senior partners at work and has a recommendation of an alternative, holistic cancer doctor in Bristol who might be worth a visit.

This time it's me that's sceptical. Gillian says she's paying for the consultation so I can jolly well get over myself and go. That's me told.

**3 February 2011 – North Hampshire Hospital, Basingstoke**

Had a thick, sticky goo injected up my bum and told to hold it in while they x-rayed. The bowel surgery has healed well and I could have the reversal now but for the chemo. I suppose this counts as a good day.

**4 February 2011 – Egham**

How depressing that size, cleanliness and accessibility of a toilet would be the deciding factors when choosing a pub for lunch. I don't tell Alison this when I suggest we meet at The Barley Mow. She thinks I like the food there. Neither do I tell her that The Bag doesn't seem too keen on any foods. I talk about the imminent arrival of Colin and my referral to an alternative, holistic doctor in Bristol. She says she'll take me. I think I'd like that. Finally we'll have our Thelma and Louise trip, she says.

**5 February 2011**

In an attempt to show Neil my days are productive and to distract me from scary online chemo forums, I made a peanut butter cake. A recipe from a colostomy bag website. Tasted disgusting. Straight in the bin. Cutting out the middle-man of bowel and Bag. Then fell down a rabbit-hole of Alison's letters as I hunted for that vegetarian recipe she promised. Don't think she ever did send it but I had a lovely time losing myself in her world.

**7 February 2011**

Picked up Colin this morning. This must be what true love feels like. We've had a flurry of visitors bearing gifts as if we'd just had a baby. Just taking him for a walk makes me feel human again. I can tell Neil is smitten too. I can't stop looking at him (Colin, not Neil). Love love love.

**9 February 2011**

Colin is introducing me to a whole new breed of people. Dog walkers. I know their dogs' names but not theirs, and they don't know mine. We chat about the weather and how marvellous our dogs are and then we move on. The Bag is camouflaged by my dog-walking coat. But better than that, these people don't even know I have cancer.

**10 February 2011**

Just read yesterday's entry. If you'd told me a year ago that the highlight of 2011 would be the shared pros and cons discussion of poo bags and worming tablets I'd have said 'let the cancer take me now'. But the unconditional, bountiful love of a dog means I'm glad to still be here.

*My contribution to the art auction*

**10 February 2011**

Dear Brian

I apologise if everything you read is an echo. I'm due to see you tomorrow so no doubt I'll have told you all my news. Might be best if you use this letter to practise your origami – turn it into a swan, crane or some other pointy-nosed creation.

Talking of origami, perhaps it's time for you to take up a new hobby.

New experiences help us grow, bring joy to our lives... and all such other spiritual twaddle! I used to work with a girl who told her team to imagine they had five pebbles in their pockets, removing one each time they went outside their comfort zone. Ideally, by the end of each week, their pockets would be empty but their lives full of new experiences. I know this is all very well but there is something reassuringly cosy and familiar about being right, bang in the centre of your own comfort zone. I say this as someone who's recently been catapulted out of hers, but more of that later. First let's talk about your comfort zone. As you've spent most of 2010 outside of yours, I thought you would be more than 'comfortable' to continue that into 2011 – in the form of a new hobby perhaps?

Of course, my new hobby suggestion isn't without selfish motivation. What I really need you to do is take up art, throw together a couple of canvasses, sign them as Van Gogh or maybe Warhol (depending on your style) and donate them to the Special Yoga charity art auction. As I mentioned at the end of last year, I've volunteered to help organise this extravaganza while I'm waiting for my next big career to present itself. You may not have had me down as an art connoisseur but I did used to work opposite Tate Modern!

At the first committee meeting, the chairwoman produced a list of last year's donating artists: Hirst, Emin, Scarfe, to name a few. These pieces had been given by the artists at the personal requests of the committee members. I began to wonder whether a signed photo of Peter Purves and Petra was going to cut it.

If I thought I was out of my comfort zone in my corporate working life, I was about to experience a whole new low. The meeting went something like this:

Chairwoman: 'Does anyone know Roman Abramovich? Because his girlfriend, Dascha, is very big on the Russian art scene.'

Committee Member 1: 'One of my best friends is about to start working in Dascha's office. I'll ask her to get her involved.'

Chairwoman: 'We've got Kirsty Allsop and Gaby Roslin doing the auctioneering, so the paparazzi will be there but obviously only Harpers and Tatler will be allowed into the event. I'll let them know. We're having drinks tomorrow. And Sienna Miller was supposed to come last year. Paparazzi around all evening. Be great if we could actually get her to turn up this year.'

Committee Member 2: 'I live next door to Savannah, her half-sister, and we're having breakfast this week, so I'll ask her to get Sienna along.'

Chairwoman: 'Of course, the trouble with the celebrities is they never put their hands in their pockets'

At last, my moment.

'Twiggy was at a charity art auction I attended recently, and her friends bid £20,000 for a Bailey photo of her,' I offered.

'Oh, you know Bailey? Fabulous. Get him to donate.'

I was trying to say no, but it was too late. She thought I knew David Bailey. Oh Brian, you don't know him, do you? And I wouldn't mind but they're not even a cancer charity.

Joining the committee wasn't a pebble I'd taken out of my pocket, it was a sodding, huge boulder.

Later I came across these wise words from Osho in an essay 'Amateurs & Experts':

It always happens when you start new work, you are very creative, you are deeply involved, your whole being is in it. Then by and by, you become acquainted with the territory, rather than being creative or inventive you start being repetitive. This is natural, because the more skilled you become in any work, the more repetitive you become. Skill is repetitive. So all great discoveries are made by amateurs because a skilled person has too much at stake. If something new happens, what will happen to the old skill?

So here is the lesson: It is good to attain skill, but it is not good to settle with it for ever. Whenever the feeling arises in you that now the thing is looking stale, change it. Invent something, add something new, delete something old. Again, be free from the pattern – that means to be free from the skill – again become an amateur. It needs courage and guts to become an amateur again, but that's how life becomes beautiful.

The next committee meeting went something like this:

Committee Member 3 (aka me): 'Who've you had to sponsor the auction in the past?'

Chairwoman: 'We've never had sponsorship. We've never thought to ask anyone. Could you get us some, do you think?'

Committee Member 3 (aka me): 'Oh, yes. I should think so. Leave it with me.'

The amateur made a discovery!

Lots of love to you, Brian

Alison

**15 February 2011**

Got a phone call from the head nurse at the chemo unit. Tomorrow's going to be an all-day affair, so she advised a picnic and something to read. And I'll need warm clothes for afterwards. More Monty Don layers. I've got Alison's letter stashed in my bag. Ruth will babysit Colin.

Took myself off to cinema to see Black Swan. Not sure which was most traumatic – the thought of chemo or the film.

**16 February 2011 – King Edward VII Hospital, Windsor**

Neil wasn't happy to leave me at the hospital. We had words. I cried. I explained I didn't want him hanging around me and my new tribe. Was I being harsh? Do I care?

They injected me with the poison and I visualised it killing off the rogue cancer cells, just like one of my cancer websites advised. As I have no idea what the cells look like I imagined them to be Pokémon. It all felt rather pointless so I stopped. Alison's letter said to embrace a new experience but I'm not sure chemo was what she had in mind.

Donned gloves, hat and scarf before running out to the car at the end of the day. By the time I got there, my lips were numb and I had a very camp lisp. Also had a twitch in my left eye. Spent the evening waiting for other side effects to develop. Only one was a tingling mouth.

## 17 February 2011

All hell kicked off with The Bag this evening. Kept filling up. Diarrhoea. A side effect of the chemo, I assume. To and fro from the loo. Empty. Full. Empty. Full. Empty. Full.

It's 4am and I'm wide awake, rattling with steroids, anti-nausea pills, anti-inflammatories. Is this what it's like being on speed? Not sure this is the right time to embark on my druggy years.

## 18 February 2011

A lost day to wipe out sleep with crazy dreams like I'd been on a cheese-fest. Not even enough energy to dress.

## 20 February 2011

A lost weekend to sleep. All I managed was a walk to Waitrose. The cold wind got my eye twitching. The woman on the till smiled at me like I was some sort of special sympathy case. Only when I caught myself in the mirror at home did I realise she must have thought I was winking at her.

**21 February 2011**

Energy surge today. Surprised Neil by being showered and dressed by time he got home. Small steps.

**23 February 2011 – Bristol**

Today was the long-awaited Thelma and Louise road trip with Alison to Dr H in Bristol. Tiredness and concerns for The Bag made me want to cancel but I didn't.

We chatted all the way there with no need for a service station stop. But once at the clinic, I discovered The Bag had leaked. The shame. I didn't tell Alison nor Dr H. Just put on a smiley face.

It was so reassuring to talk to a doctor in a holistic way. She told me about a Hungarian treatment, trialled only on dogs, which isn't available on the NHS or even licensed in the UK.

When Alison asked how the consultation went, I told her I was considering taking Hungarian dog medicine. She snorted with laughter. I reminded her at least I wasn't mad enough to join an art auction committee.

**27 February 2011**

Dear Brian

Apologies I haven't written for a while. I've had nothing bizarre, entertaining nor crazy to tell you. Perhaps I've had my quota of funny incidents, I thought. However, as we walked back to the car in Bristol the other day, I realised how wrong I was. As you waxed lyrical about Dr H, you let slip one of the most ridiculous things I'd heard in ages.

'She said the best treatment to kill cancer cells is a mixture of Vitamin C, aspirin, and copper. Much more effective than chemo,' you said.

'Oh, sounds interesting,' I replied. 'Is she recommending it for you?'

'Well,' you muttered. 'It's only actually licensed in Hungary. For dogs. But I might give it a try.'

And right there, as we strolled in the Bristol sunshine, the craziness of life returned. Hurrah for the weird and wonderful.

While you've been pondering your dog medicine, I've spent a pleasant weekend in Sussex with my super-successful, super-untidy, best friend, Natasha. Natasha is something dynamic in media marketing and knows every glossy magazine editor, fashion photographer and beauty consultant, always managing to get us into the latest hot, new restaurant, club or fashion show, all the time looking like she's stuck in some unfortunate '90's fashion nightmare.

She can't understand why I've given up my job (and salary, more pointedly) and I can't understand how she's so successful in such a glamourous industry, but we both love each other enough to not worry about it.

Natasha's job, and fact she's married to a sports agent, means she lives a life on the edge of celebrity and so is always on the look-out for any new celebrity friend. Her big news of the weekend was that they'd just put in an offer on a house in the same village as Davina McCall. We cracked open a bottle of Bollinger to celebrate that one!

The main task of the weekend was to create 30 children's party bags. Apparently, there's much party-bag competition between the parents of the Home Counties. My godson, Natasha's eldest, recently received a bag containing a voucher for a round of golf (he's nine!). While shopping, we were distracted by Lycra and fitness DVD's, prompting Natasha to question whether her daily pack of digestive biscuits, smothered in cream cheese, would need to go if Davina is to be a neighbour.

I thought about the contrast between my healthy, happy godson and those receiving treatment at the charity, Special Yoga.

But there is little point dwelling on this comparison because, as Logan Mountstuart said, 'Life is just luck'.

After a relaxing weekend, I left to have lunch with Tea Taster.

As I departed, Natasha said, 'He's a lovely, genuine man. You're lucky to still have him in your life, you know.'

'Am I?' I asked.

'Yes,' she said. 'And you know what you need to do? Be more honest with yourself about what you really want from life. And then try harder to get it.'

'He has a girlfriend.'

'Well, he's clearly not keen if he's going to lunch with you, and don't give me all that friends shit. You have to work on want you want from life, you know. Not just leave it to luck.'

# FROM ME, TO YOU

So that's me told (and Logan Mountstuart)!

Much love

Alison

# CHAPTER TEN

## LIVING WITH THE OLD BAG

**25 February 2011**

Fell asleep in the chair this afternoon and dreamt I was having chemo. I watched myself in the blue chair, staring out of the window. Every detail was there – the hot pads wrapped in towels to warm my hands and bring the veins to the surface, the nurse ready to harpoon them. The ward was full but there was no camaraderie or friendship. All of us were alone.

I woke in a sweat and then felt I couldn't get out of the chair. I was full of fear.

At least Alison's letters keep arriving, thank God. Lifting my spirits. What has she got herself into with this art auction? I do love escaping into the madness of her world as I struggle with mine.


**26 February 2011**

Neil says I've become bitter. This morning the neighbour from across the street caught me on the drive and asked how I was. But that was it. He didn't make any other conversation, as if I was no longer human but just a cancer receptacle. He and I would have chatted about family and sports and all sorts before, but not now. He looked awkward. I felt bad for him so made an excuse to go back inside. And Neil wonders why I don't want to go out.

**27 February 2011**

I know people mean well but if another person tilts their head and looks at me with pitying eyes when they ask how I am, I'm going to knock their damned head off.

**28 February 2011**

Neil says he's taking my social life in hand. He refuses to live with a cancer ileostomy recluse.

**28 Feb 2011**

Hi Brian

I'm having panic attacks. By the hour. Turns out that getting a sponsor for the art auction is 'very welcomed' but not enough. Email from charity leader Jo this week:

'Gentle reminder – every committee member is expected to source five to six pieces of art. I know for many of you this won't be difficult so please take this as a minimum. Good luck, everyone.'

Just writing this has made me come over all sweaty.

I can't remember if I mentioned I was invited to a private art viewing at the Sir John Soane's Museum. I wanted to ingratiate myself with the friend of a friend who'd invited me as he's the owner of an art gallery and helps out with the odd charity auction, I'd been told. And right now, to be honest, I'll attend anything which has the word 'art' on the invite.

I had no idea what the exhibition was about so for moral support I took along one of my old corporate colleagues, Julian, who I knew must have a sense of humour as he'd once dated a man who looked like Ronnie Corbett.

On arrival, we were greeted by a finely spoken, bearded gentleman, who air-kissed everyone's ears. He promised we were in for an amazing treat and directed us upstairs to a candle-lit champagne reception.

The gathered group was an eclectic bunch; among them was a woman in her 80s, rocking a leather dress, a man sporting half a handle-bar moustache, and a wiry teenager in a diamanté-covered T-shirt. We were invited to walk around the house to view the art. In each room we found pieces of blown glass, all phallic in shape, randomly exhibited on sofas, cabinets and chairs.

A museum volunteer flashed his torch at one piece, commenting:

'These glass things are actually quite attractive if you can see them in the proper light. Although even in the proper light, I don't know if sticking them on a sofa is how you really should display them.'

In the middle of another room was a gravestone, engraved Poor Fanny. We were unsure as to whether this was part of the exhibition until we spotted a book for sale entitled: Fanny – Mrs Soane's Dog.

Not having seen anything I imagined was going to elevate me in the eyes of the art auction committee, I returned to the reception room with Julian to down our last dregs of champagne.

'Oh, look: there's a dragon.' Julian giggled.

'Do you mean the woman wearing too much make-up?' I replied. 'She does look a fright, doesn't she?'

'No,' Julian said. 'An actual dragon.'

I peered again. There in the middle of the room was Dragons' Den's Deborah Meaden.

It was at this point I feared that if I stayed longer, I may be tempted by the bottle labelled 'Drink Me', pass through a blown-glass penis and be confronted by the museum volunteers of Tweedledum & Tweedledee, the air-kissing Mad Hatter and the Dragons' Den Queen of Hearts, all inviting me to a tea party.

We made our excuses, dived into the closest bar and got blindingly drunk on martinis. The pursuit of art is exhausting, Brian.

Much love

Alison

**1 March 2011 – London**

Local night out with Neil and Gillian – Pygmalion. Where were the tunes? Visiting the toilet in the interval was only supposed to be a 'better safe than sorry' measure but another leak meant I was, again, changing The Bag in a public cubicle. I wanted to be home. I cannot control this bloody bag but it is controlling me. When I returned to my seat, Neil asked why I had beads of sweat on my forehead.

**2 March 2011**

More bag problems today. Leak. Change. Leak. Change. The stoma nurse said I'd be able to live a normal life with The Bag. What kind of normal does she live?

Set off to London for another night out but I know I'm kidding myself that I can do this. Half way there, I needed to get out of the car as I was having a bag episode. I started crying in the garage toilets so then there was snot and tears as well as poo. I needed to be at home so told Neil to carry on and I'd catch the train back. Couldn't bear to spoil everyone's fun. Arrived home and crawled into bed.

**3 March 2011**

Neil organised dinner out – 4 of us. Trying not to let The Bag control me but I didn't want to be there. It leaked this afternoon and I was dreading it would happen again. Someone asked how I was and I started my rehearsed chemo debrief: tired, nauseous, hands so cold I have to wear gloves to open the fridge. Suddenly I heard, 'Oh let's talk about something more jolly. On Guardian Soul Mates I'm the dater with the most views this week.' I thought it must be someone at another table but it was actually one of us. I am officially a bore. Feel insignificant in my own life.

**4 March 2011**

Have to sort out The Bag. This leaking can't be right?

My skin is becoming sore too. I hate The Bag more than cancer. Life is isolating enough – with no work, every trip out an infection warzone and boring everyone to death with my ailments – without the looming threat of daily poo leak.

*When I need inspiration,*
*I always look at this.*

**5 March 2011**

Hi Brian

The charity art auction committee is up in arms!

Sam Cam has changed her availability and so they're changing the date from 9th May to the 16th. To you and me, Brian, this gives little cause for concern. To the art auction committee, this is a scheduling nightmare.

A flurry of e-mails followed the news, culminating in this one:

Very good she's given an alternative date. We probably have no option but just thought I should flag that the 16th – as it's the Monday – will be the busiest day in Cannes so will preclude anyone coming from the film world. Susie xxx

Have I missed something about the Special Yoga charity? To my mind, it's a small organisation doing amazing work for children in North-West London. But to the art auction committee, it seems it's a charity somewhere on a par with UNICEF, Médecins Sans Frontières and Barnardo's. Or is it actually that the members of the committee are going to be at Cannes themselves and are concerned about leaving the art auction in the more than incapable of hands of non-art-producing Committee Member No 3? (As well as missing a night out with Sam Cam.)

We have another meeting/personal humiliation hour on Monday so let's see how I get on. Do you think mentioning my encounter with Deborah Meaden and the glass penises will help or hinder my credibility?

Anyway, enough about me, Brian. I feel we need to focus on you today. I heard this story when I was in India and it's really stuck, so I'm going to share it with you.

In a village lived a woman with her baby son. The woman had little money and lived a simple life.

In the field behind the house was a beautiful white horse. The woman loved the horse. Every

day she fed it, going out into the field and
nuzzling her face into its neck.

One day, the emperor arrived at the village and
saw the stunning horse and took it for himself,
ignoring the woman's pleas. The woman wept. Her
neighbours took pity on her.

'You loved the horse so much,' they said. 'It
is such bad luck for you that the emperor wanted
it for himself.'

'It may be bad luck, it may be good luck,' said
the woman. 'We don't know yet as we don't know
the end of the story.'

The years passed and the woman's son grew up
into a fine young man. The woman's simple life
continued but not a day passed when she didn't
miss the beautiful, white horse.

One day, while sitting in the garden, she heard
a rumbling noise. As the noise grew louder, she
saw her beautiful, white horse galloping
towards her, followed by 50 younger horses. The
horses set themselves down to graze in her
field.

'You are so lucky,' the woman's neighbours said.
'You can breed these horses and make a lot of
money for you and your son.'

'It may be good luck, it may be bad luck,' said
the woman. 'We don't know yet as we don't know
the end of the story.'

Over the next few years, the woman and her son made a lot of money from their horse breeding business and travelled extensively.

One day, as her son worked with the horses, she heard a terrible scream. One of the horses had thrown her son from its back, and in the commotion, the other horses had trampled over him. He was so badly injured the doctor said he would never walk again. The woman wept as she thought of her son spending the rest of his life in a wheelchair.

'This is such bad luck. Your son is so badly injured,' said her neighbours.

'It may be bad luck, it may be good luck,' said the woman. 'We don't know yet as we don't know the end of the story.'

For the next couple of years, the woman looked after her son and continued to run the business. Every day, she felt sad that her son would not have the life she had hoped for him.

Then a terrible war broke out. All the young men were called up to fight. The war was bloody and many lost their lives. Families were torn apart and hearts broken.

As the woman's son was in a wheelchair, he was not needed for the war effort.

'You are so lucky,' the neighbours said. 'Your son will not go to war. He will not die.'

'It may be good luck, it may be bad luck,' said the woman. 'We don't know yet as we don't know the end of the story.'

I know you think only negative things have come from your cancer: it spoiling your life, inflicting unwanted anxiety on Neil, causing upset for those you love. But I think some real positives have come from it too. Without your illness, I would never have started writing to you, and so I would never have discovered our friendship. I have been lucky enough to observe and learn that from the darkest places can come resilience, humour and compassion. I would also never have found out how wonderful letters are, giving voice to hopes and fears, allowing true selves to be heard – that is a gift you have given me.

So, while you can't make the last nine months go away or change any of the outcomes, you can perhaps take comfort in all the wonderful things you have discovered about yourself and allowed others to discover about themselves.

Much love

Alison

**5 March 2011– North Hampshire Hospital, Basingstoke**

My stoma has changed shape, according to the stoma nurse: another side effect of the chemo. There are lots of different-shaped and -sized bags available, so I came away with a selection, plus a large box of adhesive patches. The nurse said to be patient – things will improve. Alright for her, she doesn't live with a stoma.

# CHAPTER ELEVEN

## I'M HAVING A PARTY – IN BED

**7 March 2011**

Hi Brian

The reason for the Ken Dodd comedy notepaper will become apparent but first let me update you on the art auction as, quite frankly, it has taken over my life.

My relentless quest continues. I'm stalking the friend of the friend who hosted the exhibition at the Sir John Soane's Museum, although I'm not sure I want a glass penis donated.

While others are shipping in art from around the globe, I'm still pinning my hopes on Peter Purves and his signed photo of Petra. And that's it. That's my update. Hopeless.

You remember we talked about my ex-man's recent offer to work together on a consultancy project? Well, I called him and we arranged to meet. (I can't call him 'my man' any more when he's clearly not been that for months, so he's now 'ex-man'.) It was not without ulterior motive as I wondered whether he may be persuaded to be a sponsor for the art auction or indeed reveal a vast art collection that I'd failed to spot on my visits to his house.

Sensibly, we met in town, both stressing that we had important meetings to go to afterwards. I felt quite anxious on the day but took a deep breath and headed off. As I am slowly learning, there's always something or someone looking after us, and it turned out I need not have felt nervous at all.

We met with a hug and a peck on the cheek and then I noticed he had tried to do something trendy with his hair. Unfortunately for him, this follicle transformation had left him bearing a very strong resemblance to Ken Dodd. I relaxed.

The meeting went well but I know I don't want to work with him in the cut and thrust of corporate world. Nor do I want to spend any time looking at his hair. So, I said thank you but no thank you, and it felt good.

Funny, isn't it, how time moves us along and heals so much. We just need patience and trust. He was never the one for me, was he?

Much love

Alison

**8 March 2011**

Chemo week. Bag is behaving and I have some energy. I experimented with salad over the weekend. What has my life become? Seems lettuce can go on the 'eat' list, unlike the new super-green nutrient drink, which cost me a fortune and runs straight through me, lighting up The Bag neon green. I'll give it to Alison; she needs all the nutrients she can get in her pursuit of art.

**9 March 2011 – King Edward VII Hospital, Windsor**

I didn't want to wake up today. Chemo. Go in feeling well and come out feeling dreadful.

I recognised a few of the faces. One chap, Shazad, looked over when I laughed out loud at today's letter. I passed it over.

'She's dodged a bullet with that Ken Dodd chap,' he chuckled. 'You got any more of these?' I said I'd bring some in next time.

**11 March 2011**

Post chemo days are here again. Out come the gloves to open the fridge. Warm drinks only. Wrap up when I go out. Steroid-induced sleepless nights. Wandering around the house like a ghost. And then knocked over by crippling fatigue.

Poor Neil is fielding telephone calls asking how I am. I know people mean well but what the hell can I say to the question How are you? I only have a head full of cruel replies. I cannot predict my moods from one day to the next.

**15 March 2011**

What is it with this damned chemo-fatigue? Neil suggests I look on websites for help. I think the websites need re-writing.

Cancer Research UK website says fatigue leads to:

- Lack of energy – ~~you may just want to stay in bed all day~~ *you'll have no option but to observe your life disappear into a long line of days in bed.*
- Feeling 'I just cannot be bothered to ~~do much~~ *brush my teeth'.*
- ~~Problems sleeping~~ *You will wonder why sleep evades you when only yesterday you'd've been considered for the Olympic Sleep Team.*
- ~~Finding it hard to get up in the morning~~ *Morning? They still a thing?*
- Feeling anxious or depressed. *Uh huh.*

- Pain in your muscles – ~~you may find it hard to climb stairs or walk short distances~~ *You may find it impossible to get from bed to the toilet. Embrace the commode.*
- Being breathless after doing small tasks, like having a shower ~~or making your bed~~ *Under no circumstances bother with making your bed.*
- Finding it hard to concentrate, even just watching TV or talking to a good friend *and worse, sobbing at the TV – especially at the adverts.*
- ~~Finding it hard to think clearly or make decisions easily~~ *That all went a long time ago.*
- Loss of interest in doing things you usually enjoy – *eating, drinking, friends, family, laughing, reading, films, gardening... I could go on.*
- ~~Negative feelings about yourself and others~~ *If you don't feel negative about everything in your life by this point, you're not doing it right.*

**17 March 2011**

Dear Brian

Apologies for the brevity of this letter but I have no time to write (which may be handy timing as Neil says you have no energy to even stay awake at the moment).

I am finally, I think, on the trail of some decent art. Don't want to say too much in case

I jinx it but I'm meeting a man in a hotel lobby and I'm assured great things will follow.

If you never hear from me again you can assume I've been kidnapped for my organs, and great things didn't follow (other than for the organ recipients).

Much love

Alison

## 27 March 2011 – Ruth's house

Lunch round at Ruth's today. Neil all muscles in his tight top, looking fit – just been for a run. And Ruth looking her usual stylish self.

I sat there in my smock top, over shirt, over T-shirt, over vest. God, I was hot.

## 30 March 2011 – Kind Edward VII Hospital, Windsor

Chemo session No 3. Will this be the last? Mr C said 3 to 6. Maybe 3 will be my lucky number? The Bag could be gone in time for summer. Shazad was there. I gave him the art auction letter. I didn't think it was that funny but he clearly did. Tears streaming down his face. He passed it on to the woman in the next chair who snorted when she laughed as she read. She introduced herself as Natalia and said she had a niece in Poland who is very good at art and maybe she'd donate something. Pity I don't plan on being here again. Nice to have found a few chemo buddies though. Nice not to feel like the odd one out.

**31 March 2011**

Dear Brian

Sorry I haven't written for a couple of weeks but I've had a hangover. Tea Taster has dumped his girlfriend (she retaliated by dumping a vase of water over his head, said vase having moments before contained the bunch of flowers he'd given her along with the news he no longer wanted to date her). Tea Taster and I now seem to have moved onto the 'let's get drunk together' stage (hence the hangover). Last weekend saw me taking him back to mine on a night bus – never let it be said I'm not a classy bird.

Apparently, they don't have night buses in Dorset, so this was a new experience for him!

This latest hangover has seen me out of action for a few days. I had to e-mail the charity to tell them I wouldn't be at the committee meeting because I had a sick bug. (Is it OK to lie to a charity if it's to stop them thinking you're a complete lush?) In an attempt to recover, I've been on the sofa watching DVDs. I even watched something with subtitles. However, now I know you're sharing my letters to make friends at chemo I feel under pressure to get writing again.

Between my DVD binge, I found this quote:

'Eventually, I sickened of people, myself included, who didn't think enough of themselves to make something of themselves – people who did only what they had to do and never what they could have done. I learned from them the infected loneliness that comes at the end of every misspent day. I knew I could do better'– Mark Twight: Kiss or Kill.

So, I've got my hungover arse off the sofa and here I am writing a letter. Surely, no day is misspent when a letter to you is the outcome?

But I know what you're really interested in – my art updates.

The further I get into the art world, the more out of my comfort zone I am. I feel stuck between the looming and seemingly inevitable epic fail of zero art and the increasingly tempting, but equally humiliating, resignation from the committee. Even when I think I may be getting close to some kind of piece, I still feel like a fool.

The Sir John Soane's Museum friend of a friend agreed to meet. Little did I know we would spend our time speaking in tongues.

First, he asked if I had a link to any of the collecting families. I said I didn't think so.

'Not even the Sackvilles?' He guffawed.

'I don't think so.'

Sackvilles, Brian? Who the hell are the Sackvilles? I mentioned a couple of the trustees are in private equity so may have connections. This isn't true but I couldn't lose credibility at such an early stage.

'But you do have a FarwarParis?' he asked, thumbing through an auction catalogue he'd brought along filled with Picassos, Monets and Miros.

I'm not actually sure if he did say 'FarwarParis' but it was something that sounded like that.

'Every auction needs a FarwarParis,' he told me.

FarwarParis, Brian! What's a bloody FarwarParis?

'This Picasso was a marvellous one in this auction,' he said, pointing to something colourful in the catalogue. 'What's your FarwarParis?'

I was crippled with embarrassment, knowing that whatever I said would be wrong. So I hedged my bets with, 'Well, that's where you come in...'

'Ah, yes, I see,' he laughed. 'OK. I'll speak to a few people and see what I can do. It'll be at a pinch but you never know.'

Obviously, at this stage, I'm grateful for anything but I don't imagine many heads will turn at the committee when I rock up with a FarwarParis!

I left work over 12 months ago and so far I've achieved a big, fat nothing. I have to succeed at this art hocus pocus otherwise what am I doing with my life?

If nothing else, this project is a lesson in the value of connecting and how, without the support others, you never really get anywhere. However, I'm not sure the world of art, FarwarParis and charities is the way for me to go. I feel like a fool. All the time.

I need to find my true passion, I guess. One that makes me feel good about myself!

I certainly wasn't feeling good about myself when I popped into a local shop the other day and asked about a dress hanging in the window

'Yes,' said the assistant. 'It's lovely, isn't it? Why don't you try it on? It's a large size so should be fine.'

A LARGE Brian, a LARGE.

And to make it worse, I was wearing a fitted coat, showing off my little figure, I thought.

Needless to say, I've existed on lettuce leaves ever since and have practically worn out my Davina McCall fitness DVD.

So that's my week, Brian. Started with a hangover and ends with a three stone weight gain.

Much love from Big-Al

**2 April 2011**

Got an email from Alison with an invite to her art auction on Monday 16th May.

'Brian, if you feel up to it, I'd love if you and Neil could come. Bring the bag.'

Wonder if there will be any celebrities there.

**7 April 2011**

Read Alison's letter again today. I needed a distraction. It really cheered me up – especially the story of the FarwarParis. I laughed so loudly Colin barked. Shazad would enjoy this one.

**12 April 2011**

Refusing to be hopeful/excited/giddy about tomorrow's oncologist appointment. But I do have a good feeling.

End of chemo.

Schedule reversal operation.

Bag gone.

Job done.

And a good news text from Alison too. Seems she's found not 1 but 2 FarwarParis: a Matisse and a Picasso – how fabulous.

**13 April 2011 – King Edward VII Hospital, Windsor**

The oncologist wants me to carry on with the chemo. I am responding well, he says. So The Bag gets to stick around for longer. As soon as I think I see a chink of light, it goes dark again. Seems 3 isn't my lucky number.

# CHAPTER TWELVE

## NOW, WHERE DID I PUT MY LIFE?

**16 April 2011**

Hi Brian

Miracles do happen.

I'm knee deep in art. Can you believe it? I've been catapulted from zero pieces to hero pieces. Mr FarwarParis has gone above and beyond and come up with a Dali and an Emin, as well as the Picasso and Matisse (they're some sort of artist proof sketch things but who cares – I am officially an art collector/sourcer/person and have finally earned my place round the committee meeting table). And that's not all. I have also managed to secure a painting from Charming Baker (a favourite artist of Damien Hirst but, more importantly, the best friend of Tea Taster's brother-in-law – can't believe Tea Taster remembered my art plight and helped out) and something from a bloke called Dan who has had some exhibitions in Mayfair. I'm also working on another lead – someone who paints with Prince Charles.

Of course, there's still time for you, Brian. If you wanted, in a quiet moment on the chemo ward, feel free to whip out your sketch book. But I imagine you're less than delighted to still be going to chemo so you might just want to scribble black ink across the page. I can always pass it off as art therapy, so go for your life (maybe go for your life isn't the right phrase. Sorry)

But on a serious note, while I am delighted I've managed to acquire some art, it really has taught me a big life lesson – don't put your hand up for things that you know nothing about. It's just not worth the panic attacks.

But your three-chemo session news got me thinking about that very number and its magical qualities – although not so magical for you, it seems. So many things work on the principle of threes – a story has a beginning, middle and end; advertisers use three adjectives to describe a product; pictures are divided into thirds to create pleasing compositions. So, it should come as no surprise that life, if we let it, also orders itself in this way.

Here is my week of threes:

I went to lunch with a friend. Her three young kids gave me my very belated Christmas presents – a tea towel, a door stop and a ceramic dog filled with boiled sweets. I could understand this rather odd collection of gifts had the children chosen them themselves but they hadn't; they'd been chosen by their mother. I've known my friend since our school days and never in that time has she seen me drying up dishes, struggling to keep doors open or gorging myself on bags of Sherbet Lemons and Cola Cubes! Very odd.

Earlier this week, I made three attempts to frame a picture. For Easter, I'd bought Tea Taster a rather tasteful, small pencil drawing and needed a frame. As he lives in a Georgian house, I'd cleverly purchased a Georgian-style frame on eBay. It arrived in a box the size of my car and the drawing looked completely lost in such an ornate, bulky monstrosity. Embarrassed by my poor choice (what with me now being a person of the art[NE3]s), I ran to the shops to buy a simple, dainty frame. I found one in the charity shop, bought it, took it home, dropped it, broke the glass and threw it away. This morning I found myself in a framing shop – where I should have been from the start. Third time lucky!

My third three was spying three men dressed as clowns in the high street followed by three dogs.

# FROM ME, TO YOU

Talking of threes, there were three of us having Sunday lunch at Tea Taster's last weekend, one of whom was his twinkly-eyed mother. Over lunch, I began to understand why I like her so much. Tea Taster had whipped up a roast and, perhaps in an effort to impress his mother (or indeed me, his new girlfriend!), had topped it off with 'proper' gravy. (Usually his gravy is four parts water, one part marmite.) Talk of gravy encouraged his mum to mention her beach hut lover.

'David always makes the gravy,' she said. 'He can make it beautifully. He uses those gravy granules. Oh, it is delicious.'

This reminded me of Tea Taster's stories of his childhood meals. His mum's cookery pièce de résistance was the surprise plate. This was a plate of anything – grapes, sausage, crisps, chocolate, jelly, nuts, tomatoes. The only criteria was that none of the component foods should complement each other in any meal-type way.

In a conversation earlier in the day, she'd been talking about her house in the 70s.

'We had a new kitchen put in,' she'd said. 'It was when everyone was having kitchen appliances but I didn't like them, so we just had a sink.'

A woman after my own heart. Do you think this is why Tea Taster is attracted to me? Because I remind him of his mother?

What I wasn't so keen on was her well-intentioned question about what I was doing for work these days. Suddenly, the rule of three was back in play. I told her about being asked to go back to my old job, or a less well-paid version of it; of an ex-colleague asking me to do some consultancy work for his firm but advising me to double my proposed daily rate if I wanted to be taken seriously; and finally, about attending a networking event, bumping into an ex-client, him asking what I was doing, me fudging it, and him offering me some work 'if I could fit it in'!

'But is that really where you see yourself, back in the corporate world of politics, targets and stress?' she asked. Turns out you don't need a kitchen full of appliances to know what's important in life.

The Latin saying, *omne trium perfectum*, would have us believe everything that comes in threes is perfect, but your round of three chemo sessions wasn't perfect. Are these three offers of work back in corporate world perfect for me?

I suppose if all fails, I'll just get a dog and join the three clowns on the High Road. Oh, but then there'd be four...

Much love

Alison

**16 April 2011**

I am falling apart, like that old rag doll my sister used to have. Next round of chemo is cancelled as blood count too low. Want to say yippee but it's not really yippee, is it?

And then in some sort of weird act of complicity, a filling fell out. Booked an emergency dental appointment but as my white cells are in such short supply, leaving me prone to infection, I can only have a temporary filling with no injection. Have swapped chemo persecution for dental persecution.

**18 April 2011 – Dentist**

I now have a cavity filled with what is essentially chewing gum. Bought a doughnut as a treat and ate it secretly. I never eat doughnuts – wtf!

**19 April 2011**

White blood cell counting has replaced sheep. Doesn't work – I lie for hours weighing up the pros and cons. Lots of cells equals more chemo with the nausea and crippling fatigue. A few cells equals following the sheep over the cliff.

## 20 April 2011

Instead of the chemo-ward blue chair with one of Alison's letters, I'm sitting with the real Alison in my garden, admiring the rhododendrons. She wondered how one type of plant could produce such a diverse riot of colour. I wondered whether I'd even see next year's. I didn't say this out loud.

Very flattered non-green-fingered Alison appreciated the garden. Nice to think I'm still good at something, even if it is only weeding.

## 29th April 2011

The great day has arrived. Royal Wedding. Colin wore a celebratory fascinator – looked better than Beatrice and Eugenie. We had a small party outside – infection-safe-zone for me. Nice to meet Alison's sister, Jane. Two zany peas in a pod. Her red, white and blue trifle went down very well.

Good to hear Alison and Tea Taster are officially an item. Wonder when we'll get to meet him?

## 30 April 2011

Unexpected email arrived today.

Congratulations! You have been allocated some of the greatest tickets on earth!

It's from the London 2012 Olympic ticketing team, confirming my application has been processed. It's over a year away. Wonder if I'll still be alive then?

**3 May 2011**

Hi Brian

Nothing philosophical or numerical today – can't be churning those out too often. But I do have three rhododendron facts: they're the national flower of Nepal, their flowers can be poisonous to animals and eating the honey of bees who've collected their pollen can make you ill.

In all the excitement of the royal wedding celebrations, I didn't tell you about my own trip to the Abbey.

I'd had a text from my Traveling-Wilbury friend, Flora, saying she was camping outside the Abbey and would I pop by. She had rocked up four days before to secure her spot and was with the other royal wedding fans. She sat, majestic, on a camping seat bedecked in Union Jack bunting. Most people had tents, but not Flora.

'Just a sleeping bag and umbrella.' She laughed.

She suggested we go for a coffee and as we picked our way through the camp, she told me she'd been interviewed by 25 TV crews, feeding them lines such as, 'I think countries with monarchies tend to be more stable', 'I've come all the way from Australia for this' and 'I was here for Princess Diana's wedding'. None of these were true but, along with the rest of the nation, Flora had got rather carried away with wedding fever.

However, it turned out that Flora had news for me that indeed could rival the excitement of a royal wedding.

I was introduced to Flora about nine years ago. She is, by profession, a nurse but, for the last 15 years, has been cycling and hitchhiking her way around the world. When she needs money, she takes on nursing work. Her cycling and hitch-hiking trips are peppered with romances. When I first met her, she was dating a man from Leeds who had picked her up in his Sainsbury's lorry. They claimed they had so much in common, both being keen travellers: Flora travelling round the globe, Sainsbury's man travelling up and down the M1. I never know where and when Flora will pop up next but whenever I spend time with her, I feel as if a wave of 'life is good' has washed over me. Flora is fearless, with endless curiosity. Observing her life so often highlights the gaps in my own.

In the café, she told me she had some very exciting news. So exciting, in fact, I was only the third person to be told. I assumed she was about to become a grandma but when she followed up with the line, 'And I'll probably be entering public life in the future', I knew I'd guessed wrong. She furtively looked over her shoulder before continuing.

I've become a ...arian,' she said.

'A what?'

'I live on light,' she whispered. 'I'm a ...arian.'

I had no clue what she was talking about.

'I've become a breatharian. I live on light. I haven't eaten or drunk anything for 35 days.'

Flora explained she'd spent the last month on a no-eating-or-drinking course in Italy and was now existing on fresh air. She doesn't know yet whether she will want to enter public life in the future with her 'interesting, science-conflicting life-style' but if she does her son has agreed to be her PR manager. Due to fear and prejudice, she says she is not telling anyone of her decision other than her son, her current boyfriend and me.

As the waitress approached, Flora put her finger to her lips.

'I'll have camomile tea,' I said.

'And I'll have a hot chocolate,' said Flora.

What! Had Flora not spent the last ten minutes telling me she doesn't eat or drink? In my naivety, I had assumed this to include hot chocolate.

'It's to be sociable,' she whispered. 'I don't want people to guess.'

Flora, sipping her hot chocolate and speaking in whispers, told me about all things Breatharian and her transformed life. I couldn't believe what I was hearing but Flora is quite convinced that she, and hundreds like her, can defy nature and live the rest of their lives on air. We both ignored the elephant in the room — or should I say the empty hot chocolate mug.

Finally, it came time to say goodbye, partly because my head was swimming and partly because I was hungry and feared if I ordered a sandwich,

Flora would order a full roast dinner. To be sociable.

When you think you've heard everything, something comes along to remind you you'll never hear it all. Life is full of interesting people if you listen out for them. I guess this is what letter writing is doing: making me stop, listen and pay attention. Although I have to say, the favourite part of my new hobby is this, right now, as I sit here, glass of wine in hand and, just for an hour, do nothing but write. It's like I'm in a trance or a meditation. Time stops and I'm transported to another place, a place where I'm truly truly content. What a gift.

But now I must go, Brian. I have a pack of light in the fridge that will go off if I don't eat it today!

Much love

Alison

# CHAPTER THIRTEEN

## WAKE UP AND SMELL THE ROSES

**14 May 2011**

Bought EuroMillions ticket to give me a chance to buy something at Alison's auction. If this fatigue carries on, I'll be one of those people doing a telephone bid. They'll think they've got an oligarch dialling in.

**15 May 2011**

Didn't win the EuroMillions so no Matisse or Picasso for me. Will I be able to afford the FarwarParis, I wonder?

What I really need to know is what the parking is like and whether there are toilets.

I haven't told Alison how I feel about such a grand event with my dodgy white blood count and The Bag. It's important I go, not just for her but for our friendship. Feel I owe her. It's a big thing. She needs it to be a success

**16 May 2011 – Westbourne Grove, London**

Alison's charity art auction evening.

Much celeb spotting – saw Sam Cam, Gabby Roslin & my favourite, Kirsty Allsop. Sam Cam was tottering in high heels in a smart cropped-leg navy trouser suit. Kirsty had on some mumsy floral dress and was in need of a trip to the hairdresser's but has flawless skin. Gabby Roslin, so beautifully groomed on TV, looked like she might have left the house in a rush!

Oh, yes and then there was the art! An Andy Warhol went for £36,000! I was outbid by Kirsty Allsop's boss on a limited-edition print, which was just as well considering the price. I did get a print by Robi Walters in the silent auction. I am really happy with it as it's a little unusual. It's called London Star and will shine very brightly in my study. Robi was there himself, sporting a very nice mustard jacket but that wasn't up for auction, he said.

The Bag behaved. I was rather warm in my 4 layers of clothes and the many adhesive patches I'd used in a bid to keep the damn thing in place, but it didn't leak. Hurrah.

**17 May 2011**

My contribution to the art auction £125. Total raised £65,000.

**18 May 2011 – King Edward VII Hospital, Windsor**

Back to chemo. Let's get this poison into my veins. I take a couple of letters in my bag for Shazad but it's all new faces. Alison is my only friend today (and, of course, Flora the Breatharian. Really? Would you?).

**19 May 2011**

Wipe-out sleep.

# Me?

## Fabulous?

### Not tonight!

**17 May 2011**

Hi Brian

Thank you so much for coming to the art auction, and putting your hand in your pocket. Feedback from the committee is that it really isn't on to attend such an event and not try to buy something at least. I won't name names but those sitting on their hands are certain to be black-balled next year!

I am doubly grateful for your attendance, having read your recent blog post. I was upset when you talked about not doing so well lately and your pesky white blood count. You mentioned that coming to the art auction was the first time you and The Bag had done a 'social with strangers'. When we first discussed the event, I never expected you to be well enough to attend but more recently you've been doing so well it seemed, to my mind, easy for you to be there.

Wrapped up in my own world, I never considered how you felt.

There were a number of other hidden struggles in the room that night. Claire, with her stellar successful career, accepting invites to everything as she can't bear the loneliness of her single life. My friend, Dinah, bidding with her married lover, him buying a picture to take home to his wife. Samantha Cameron remembering her son, Ivan, who was a regular visitor to the charity. And, of course, we were all there to support children whose lives are so much more of a struggle than our own. But everyone, from time to time, struggles, struggles that so often aren't obvious to others.

I too had had my own struggle that evening. Everything had got off to a great start and I was smug, knowing my friends would be impressed and think I was fabulous. Buoyed up by this, and by my maxi-dress, I swanned around, champagne in hand, greeting everyone with a big smile and air kisses galore. Imagine my glee when the photographer from Tatler asked if he could take my photo, and took my name.

Well into the evening I came upon Tina. Tina advises the charity and I'm rather in awe of her as she's super successful, super nice and super adept at giving advice in a helpful and constructive way (unlike me, who tends to spend most meetings saying 'You've done what?' and

'Oh my God!'). We have become friendly and I'm on a mission to impress her so she will stay my friend forever. As we chatted, a girl approached, all smiles and familiar hellos. Being adept in the art of blagging, I gushed about how lovely it was to see her. She very obviously knew me and it became clear we had met before but I could not think who she was. She introduced me to her friend, so requiring me to introduce her to mine.

'And can I introduce you to Tina...' I began but as the words left my mouth I had a flashback. I did know the girl. We'd met by a swimming pool in a garden. A garden in Hampshire. A garden attached to Tina's house.

The girl I was introducing to Tina was her very own daughter.

Goodness knows what my face must have looked like but Tina covered my embarrassment by making some comment about not recognising anyone without her glasses. Some people are just naturally classy, aren't they? I scuttled away, making my excuses, saying something about photographs, glossy magazines and more champagne. Smug me was very much put back in her box.

Must away now, Bri, as I have a friend coming to stay and we're going to drink champagne in my backyard, which I like to pass off as a garden. You are so lucky to have your lovely garden when the weather is like this. Make sure you're enjoying it.

Take care

Much love

Alison

**25 May 2011**

The smell of the roses in the garden this evening was so intense. Was my sense of smell this strong before? Have I found one positive from chemo? Must text Alison and tell her that I am indeed enjoying my garden.

**26 May 2011- Hillier's Garden Centre, Windlesham**

Today's task – bought plants. Too knackered to plant them.

**29 May 2011**

Spent a very pleasant afternoon re-reading some of Alison's letters. They do make me laugh. There's no pity, no obligation to respond nor explain how I feel – it's just me and the letters and yet, somehow, I don't feel alone when I'm reading them. At least it seems she's getting her love life sorted. Wonder if I can help with her career-life?

Be a shame if she slipped back into corporate world now the art auction is finished. It's not like she needs to – no kids, no responsibilities. I need to encourage her to keep chasing her passion, whatever that may be. I'll invite her over for lunch for a chat.

## 2 June 2011

Alison's response to my offer of a career chat is that we should have a strategy day where we can set some personal and career goals in our new lives. Not quite what I had in mind. I guess it's all she knows when someone mentions career.

She arrived with her agenda.

1. Intro over a cup of tea and a biscuit. *I managed this.*
2. Discuss each other's strengths and weaknesses so we know how to help each other. My weakness is I have cancer. *Not sure strength is a word that applies to me anymore.*
3. Agree our objectives. *Survive another 6 months.*

I added funeral planning to the agenda. That put Alison back in her box.

We didn't find a new career. I asked what she did to relax and she said writing letters to me, so I suggested she do more of it. I wondered whether she should try some creative writing. She said she'd think about it.

**4 June 2011**

Bought a Smythson notebook and popped it in the post to Alison – somewhere for her to collect her anecdotes for letters or anything else she might write.

**5 June 2011 – Virginia Water**

Long walk round the lake with Colin today. When the steroid energy kicks in, I need to take advantage, but kept having to stop to catch my breath. Where's the man who once ran half marathons? Disappeared up his own ileostomy bag.

**6 June 2011**

Got to meet Tea Taster – Alison's 'official' new man. Never met a real live tea-taster before. Panicked by the thought of making him a cup of tea, so bought expensive loose-leaf from Waitrose and a strainer. He spat it out after 1 sip. Just a joke, he said. Handsome boy though – no wonder Alison is keen on him. One thing she has omitted to mention is he has 3 kids – a 10, a 15 and a 20-year-old. Crikey! But Colin liked him so he's OK by me.

**7 June 2011**

Hi Brian

Today's letter is all about kids – well, one kid: my four-year-old nephew who has been staying with me for a few days. And exhausted though I am by him, it's been so joyful to spend time together, me seeing the world through his eyes. And what a fabulous and fascinating place it proves to be.

And I mean, Brian, it's not like you were expecting me to write about any other kids, were you?

This was my nephew's first visit to London without his mum. He commented that my house would be nicer if I had more outdoor space for a trampoline and swings, but seemed appeased by the promise of ride on a double-decker bus (a first) and the Tube (another first). I hate public transport, especially since a friend sat on a wet seat on the Tube (and it wasn't water), but my nephew knew nothing of such things. He'd heard there were trains that travelled under the ground and buses taller than lamp posts.

Upstairs on the bus, he squealed, 'We're as high as the trees. I can see the tops of cars.'

And on the Tube, he tapped the window to check the darkness beyond was real.

'I love the underground train, Auntie Ali,' he said. 'Can we stay on all day?'

We actually spent the day at the Natural History Museum, me having promised dinosaurs. He gawped at the towering Dippy dinosaur skeleton in the hall.

'Look how long its tail is,' he said, stretching out his arms as far as they would reach. A giant replica squid was greeted with an, 'Oh my God, look at that' but best of all was the time we spent in the dinosaur exhibition. Life size, animatronic dinosaurs growled from their leafy swamps. Every child asked their parents if the models were real and every parent answered that they thought they could be. Children chatted to each other about the names of the dinosaurs, what they liked to eat and which were the predators.

We stood for ages watching these huge creatures move and roar. No fear, just fascination. We were all in a fantasy world.

Later, my nephew proudly donned a pith helmet, binoculars and explorer's backpack to join a group of children taking part in an animal hunt.

When we left, it wasn't just him who'd spent the day being over-awed and excited; I had too. I forgot I'd seen the animals many times before and that the dinosaurs were just great big puppets. I'd seen everything in a new and fresh way, and it was joyful. Picasso once said, 'Every child is an artist. The problem is how to remain an artist once we grow up.'

As adults, we often forget to connect to the child in us; we become bored with our lives, nothing fascinates us anymore and we hunt out greater and greater thrills, often to the detriment of ourselves and others.

But how do we continue to be fascinated, excited by new experiences and not scared of what others will think? How do we keep rediscovering the child within us? Can a new sport, hobby or passion take us back to being a child, I wonder?

So, here is your challenge, Brian. How will you rediscover the child in you, if only for a blissful moment?

And so OK, while we're talking 'child', I feel I need to address the elephant in the room (and don't think I don't know you've skim-read the letter to get to this bit!)

I hadn't not told you Tea Taster had kids; I just hadn't told you. You should have seen your face when he recounted the story of catching 15-year-old Alfie smoking weed and his defence being that it was OK as, unlike his friends, he doesn't steal money to buy the drugs but instead just uses the money Tea Taster gives him for babysitting his brother. My mum wonders if I know what I'm taking on (she said it with the same smugness she told me they don't need to wear Lycra for Tai Chi). And yes, the kids live with Tea Taster but that's fine. It will be fine. I mean, how hard can it be? And anyway, Scarlett's left home so it's only actually two. I'll shut up now. It's fine. Really fine. And they're lovely boys, Alfie and Billy.

Much love, Brian

Alison

## 8 June 2011 – King Edward VII Hospital, Windsor

Chemo round 5. Natalia is here but no Shazad. Not well, apparently. But then none of us are well, to be fair. Natalia's remembered the art auction and wants to know how it went. She loved hearing about Kirsty Allsop (she says she's always been jealous of her on account of her getting to spend so much time with Phil, who is Natalia's guilty pleasure).

## 17 June 2011 – Red Lion, Lightwater

My birthday. I made it.

Birthday celebration with The Bag, Neil, me, Tracy and Hamish. I said no to champagne as the fizz causes The Bag to inflate into a rock-hard balloon, and I then find it fascinating to pat and stroke it. But this was not appropriate behaviour for a restaurant apparently. Hardly seems appropriate to write in my diary either.

## 22 June 2011 – King Edward VII Hospital, Windsor

Five is my new lucky number. No more chemo. But it's not for good reasons. Apparently, my white blood cell count is too low; the skin around my fingernails is deeply cracked, which means my body is struggling generally and so cannot endure any more chemo.

The new plan is chemo tablets instead of infusions, then a scan and, if all OK, the reversal operation. Bye bye The Bag.

I did a little skip in the car park as I left. No more sitting in the blue chair. But, really, I'm kidding myself. We have failed. I haven't managed to get to the end of my chemo.

**23 June 2011**

I am still worried about the oncologist's decision to abandoned the infusions at 5 when we were initially trying for 8. He said oncology is a crude science in terms of dosage, and 8 is the maximum dose based on the strongest person. He said the stats do not take into account other factors such as allergic reactions, complications or death. Most patients only get to 4 sessions, so I've done better than average. I wondered whether the average patient gets to 4 sessions before they die or before they just stop. I didn't ask which.

**24 June 2011**

It's 3am. I'm awake. Can't even try to sleep as closing my eyes seems to speed up my thoughts, and they are all thoughts that I don't want.

Spent most of today with the toilet bowl. If it wasn't one end it was the other. Nearly fell asleep with my head down it at one point. How can I be this tired but not be asleep? And how can 24 hours last for so long? If the steroids kick in tomorrow, I will take advantage of the energy boost and get out in the garden. Do I have enough compost, I wonder? See? I said I was having thoughts I didn't want.

Maybe the oncologist was right – maybe my body has had enough. Maybe I've had enough.

# CHAPTER FOURTEEN

## TOTALLY RATTLED

**3 July 2011**

Hi Brian

I've been on holiday to Scarborough – I know, not how you expected this letter to begin! Every year, my mum organises a family holiday – usually a lovely cottage in Devon or Cornwall – and this year we were planning on doing the same, just at a different location. Or that was what I thought until I received a text from my sister, as I drove up the A1: Could you bring another room?

Seaview Villas is a decrepit Victorian building, with peeling paintwork, rotting window frames and more than a whiff of something odd: either damp or old people. The woman on reception dispensed electricity meter tokens in exchange for 50 pence pieces while at the same time dangling her hand, cigarette between fingers, out of the window. It turned out my mum had actually booked a one-bedroom flat in this 'luxury complex' with an additional room on a separate floor for herself. My sister, two-year-old niece, four-year-old nephew and I were to sleep in one room of two single beds and one double. The kids secured the singles by weeing in them on the first night.

The slot-operated electricity meter brought out the true northerner in my mum. As if 50 pence coins were being rationed in Scarborough, we could only watch TV if at least two people were viewing and no appliances could be left on stand-by, as apparently stand-by 'eats electricity' so wall sockets had to be switched off when not being used. By the end of the week, our one-bedroom four-person apartment had consumed a daily average of 30p worth of electricity. The North East England electricity board is considering us for a 'Save The Environment' case study.

If we wanted to save even more electricity we could eat at Amigo's Mexican next door. Amigo's is the sort of restaurant you see featured on Ramsay's Kitchen Nightmares. Unfortunately, Gordon hasn't yet made it to Scarborough and it took only one visit for my mum to mark it as off limits.

The sun shone on us for one day, a day spent on the beach with sweaters and donkeys. Every other day boasted the sort of weather you can expect of the North Sea coast, and we turned into those people who visit model villages and sit in greasy-spoon cafes nursing mugs of tea.

I could go on with more tales of our family holiday but I imagine you've got the general idea.

On the way home, I rewarded myself with a stop off in Suffolk to stay with my New Year friends. What a contrast! I slept in a bedroom on my own, electrical items were turned on at all times, and no one suggested I ride on a donkey. I would now like to retract everything I said in my last letter about the wonder and fascination of seeing the world through the eyes of a four-year-old. Load of old tosh. Give me a gin and tonic and adult hang-ups any day.

Much love

Alison

### 9 July 2011 – Dorset

We're in Dorset for the weekend, guests of Alison and Tea Taster at his Georgian gentleman's residence. Sarah is invited too. It's one of the few times we've been together since we first met in India. Sadly,

Colin was not given a warm welcome by Tea Taster's Jack Russell, Lizzie. Attacked him as soon as we got in. Bitch. Think we were all secretly delighted when she fell in the river on our walk. Colin didn't show any interest as we tried to hoist Mad Lizzie to safety, with Neil hanging on to Alison's ankles as she lay outstretched down the muddy river bank.

I was looking forward to dinner as I had promised myself a glass of Hassagne Montrachet, my favourite wine. Relaxed and happy, I wanted to savour that first sip. We all said cheers and I realised how much I had missed these sorts of communal moments. I put glass to mouth. Felt the chill on my lips... Ugh – my God. Metallic. Is this how all wine will taste from now on? I am a teenager again, craving the sweetness of Southern Comfort & lemonade. Of course, I told everyone how lovely it was and how much I'd missed it. And then sipped slowly. Very slowly.

**10 July 2011 – Dorset**

Five Go Mad in Dorset on a coastal walk. I'd been imagining a stroll on the prom but it seems that Alison has become sporty now she has an out-of-town boyfriend, so we yomped off to the WWII abandoned village of Tyneham.

Suddenly cancer is a very handy excuse to take rests. Once at the village, I couldn't face the return walk so Neil had to trek back to fetch the car. The others offered to stay with me, which is very nice of them but I'm sure they were just using me as a convenient excuse. Seems that Alison has also become a cook – delicious supper this evening. Whatever next?

**11 July 2011 – Dorset**

Five Go Mad in Dorset at Studland Bay. Interestingly, Tea Taster decided to take us to the part of the beach where clothing is optional. We all chose to stay fully dressed. Alison and I sat re-reading her letters, looking for the best bits. She wonders whether she can make them into short stories. This does explain the plethora of short story anthologies I spotted lying around Tea Taster's house. Nice to think she's taken me up on my suggestion she try a bit of creative writing. At least something positive has come out of our strategy day.

From her beach towel, Sarah shouted out, 'I didn't know penises came in so many shapes and sizes.' And she's supposed to be an experienced internet dater.

**17 July 2011**

Hi Brian

Thank you so much for coming down to Dorset. Sorry about the plastic spiders in your bed, the alarm clock going off at 3am and Billy's baby tooth in your porridge. I hope it hasn't put you off visiting again! Ben has had words with Alfie.

Now, you know I said I was done with art auctions? Well, it seems news of my 'expertise' has spread and I've been invited to join the art auction committee for an environmental charity. I didn't feel I could say no as the invite came from Mr FarwarParis, and I do owe him a favour.

However, I do think that I may have overplayed the whole 'I'm really into art' story. My deception is now at such a level that when I go out with people I haven't seen for a while and I recount some of the stuff I've been up to over the last few months, they say 'Oh, who'd have thought that your life would end up going down an art route?'

Going down an art route? As we both agreed on our strategy day, Bri, there's as much chance of me going down an art route as there is of me giving up designer shoes and handbags and moving to Africa to care for orphans.

However, once one has created a life based on myth and fantasy, it seems one has to carry on with it. So, on that basis, I tottered along to the Royal Academy on Piccadilly to the first committee meeting.

I was rather apprehensive because, let's face it, I don't have art contacts (well I do, but he was chairing the meeting).

I sat beside Ted, who works at Deutsche Bank and was wearing a pinkie ring. On the other side was Lucienne, who'd just completed an Ironman for the charity, and opposite was Andrew, the CEO, just back from a fundraising trip to LA with Hollywood's A-list. There was going to have to be a lot of smoke and mirrors for me to pull this one off!

But then a marvellous thing happened. It turned out that I was not the least art-knowing person in the room. Oh no, Brian, I was in fact the most art-knowing person. By the luck of the gods (or maybe just poor committee member selection) my fellow do-gooders knew bugger all about art or how to run an art auction.

The meeting was dominated by me saying things like, 'The last time I organised an art auction...', 'What one finds with artists...' and 'Whatever you do, don't invite...'

Mr FarwarParis said he had already managed to secure eight pieces of art, including a Picasso and a Matisse. (I do wonder if Mr FarwarParis actually creates these grand-masters in a shed at the bottom of his garden and uses art auctions to offload them to art-numpties like me. Probably his test is to ask if you have a FarwarParis and if you look blank and titter, he knows you haven't a clue and will be incapable of spotting his pile of potting shed fakes.)

Iron Man Lucienne asked, 'So, you have all the art we need?'

I laughed meanly and said, 'Goodness no. At my auction, we had in excess of 40 pieces. It's all a numbers game.' I'd become very blasé by this stage and completely forgotten my manners.

'We'll need an auctioneer connected to one of the main auction houses,' said Mr FarwarParis. 'And it would be good to have celebrity support. Any suggestions?'

Suddenly, the inexperienced committee came into their own, reeling off names as if they'd swallowed Tatler, Hello and Grazia.

Ruby Wax, Jeremy Clarkson, Jeremy Paxman, Tom Jones, Catherine Tate, John Cleese, Natasha Kaplinsky, Christine Bleakley, John Sargeant (very popular suggestion - hilariously funny apparently), Bruce Forsyth, Melvyn Bragg, Jeffrey Archer, Jonathan Dimbleby, Graham Norton, Nicholas Parsons (collective ahhhh) ... On and on the list went.

'My God,' I said. 'I can't believe you know so many famous people.'

'Oh, we don't know these people,' said Andrew. 'We're just listing names.'

'So how are you going to get them to come?'

'Oh, we have to know them, do we? Oh, I see. Well, that's different. So, who do we know that's connected to the charity?'

After a moment...

'Does anyone know Rory Bremner?' someone asked. 'He could just impersonate all the others.'

The meeting ended with the final agenda item — a name for the auction. Everyone was silent, even me — but as we know, I do art, not strap lines. And I could afford to be quiet as no one was going to top trump my place as 'most valuable person on the committee'.

A woman at the end of the table who'd said nothing all night other than suggesting Ruby Wax, proclaimed, 'Just off the top of my head, how about Still Life, Wildlife?'

Just off the top of her head? I don't think so. She'd been working on that one for the last two weeks. She'd probably taken holiday from work to devote herself to strap-lining.

The committee went crazy. They loved it. Best thing they'd heard all night. How lucky we are that you're on the committee, they squawked.

Suddenly, I was a nobody. A side-lined art expert.

I made my excuses and left – said I had to be somewhere fabulous with artists. No one heard – too busy debating fonts.

I had arrived at the meeting in dread I was about to be exposed as an art fraud and I left peeved that no one cared or even noticed the fraud that I am.

How fragile our egos are, Brian. If this isn't a sign I need to get my life in order I don't know what is. You were right on our strategy day – art's not really for me.

Before I sign off, I must tell you how much I'm enjoying my new notebook. What a marvellous gift you have given me. I do actually feel like a real writer now, constantly scribbling down overheard conversations, although I can see it is going to get me into trouble as I'm literally joining people at their table in cafes so I can better hear what they're saying.

The husband and wife, sitting in the cafe, were doing a crossword.

'23 down,' said the wife. 'Long-eared animal, three letters, starting with A.'

'Ant?' said the man hopefully.

'Ant?! The long-eared ant?' screeched the wife.

The husband hung his head in shame.

'Ass!' snapped the wife.

'I know I am,' said the husband. 'Sorry.'

Much love

Alison

## 14 August 2011 – Penny Hill Park

Out with Gillian. Still can't face a glass of wine. Gillian doesn't let that stop her, which makes me smile. It's the people who continue to behave as they always would that are true friends – treating me like a person rather than a cancer patient; not allowing themselves to lose touch because they don't know how to behave or what to say. Who'd have thought cancer could strengthen a friendship?

## 17 August 2011 – Penny Brohn Cancer Care, Bristol

I've been on the waiting list for Penny Brohn Cancer Care Centre for ages. I'd heard such good things about the education and care they provide but when they phoned with a late cancellation I didn't want to go. Not with The Bag. But I had a word with myself and we're here.

We are ten women and two men. I strategically placed myself half way round the welcome circle so I wasn't required to kick off the introductions. Each person told their cancer story but I didn't want to tell mine. Didn't want to say I hadn't come alone. I'd come to learn not to share. But when it came to me, I told them everything and they listened. They got it. They are like me and I am like them.

## 18 August 2011 – Penny Brohn Cancer Care, Bristol

Wow, what a lot to learn: how to eat well, manage stress, understand the immune system, exercise, secretly snooze through a meditation session. I've read books and websites telling you to do all these things but I've never really understood the science till now. I don't need to be passive with my cancer. I really can take control of my life again. This has been a good day.

## 20 August 2011

I slept so well and woke feeling positive and even a little sad to leave. We were sent on our way with a drink and sweet treat – cacao and carob brownies. Best thing I've tasted for ages and so healthy. I ate 2! And got the recipe.

Two hours later, I was cursing. Cacao and carob need to go on the avoid-food list. Who knew there were so many service stations on the M4 but thank God there are. I wished I hadn't said I'd call at Alison's on the way home but in the spirit of trying to take back control of my life I decided I wouldn't cancel. And, unexpectedly, I'm glad I didn't.

**23 Aug 2011**

Hi Brian

I know what you're thinking... another letter!
I know, I am the gift that keeps on giving.

Yesterday, I listened to a radio programme about
ice cream vans. The presenter had been
responsible for the sound effects at a Banksy
exhibition a couple of years ago. As part of
the event, he'd created chimes for a burnt-out
ice cream van.

Once the exhibit was finished, he decided to
use the chimes as his mobile ringtone. When in
public, perhaps on the train, he noticed the
ringtone caused newspapers to be lowered and
corners of mouths to turn up. He imagined
memories flooding back of the scramble to put
shoes on, panicking to get money from a parent
and running into the street to claim your 99 or
ice lolly. He told the story of when Glasgow
police played ice cream van chimes to a group
of fighting, drunken youths. As the grainy music

rang out across the angry mob, the scrapping teenagers began to laugh and the fight was over.

Every so often, the radio programme interspersed the dialogue with chimes. Each time I smiled.

So, Brian, your task for the day is to google 'ice cream chimes', listen and smile – you won't be able to help yourself. And then share your easy 'cheer-me-up' tip with friends and spread the word of the chime! There is something fascinating about how familiar sounds, images and smells can make us feel happy, even though they don't tap into any one specific memory.

But it's not just past experiences that make us smile. New ones can bring just as much mirth, as we discovered recently with Rattle Man. I know you were with me when we came across him but I wanted to re-live it as it's still making me chuckle.

We walked into the health food shop on Chiswick High Road, you keen to purchase everything you'd learnt about at Penny Brohn, and browsed the shelves, making appropriate comments: 'I love bean shoots', 'Don't talk to me about carob' and 'You're so lucky to have such a great range of health foods in west London.'

I'm sure that to the average supermarket shopper we would have sounded like complete arses, but to the average Chiswick inhabitant we fitted right in! Or we did until we succumbed to Rattle Man.

Rattle Man was perched at the back of the shop on a high stool, by the freezers. He was dressed in cheesecloth, with sequins and beads plaited into his long, wispy beard. On a table beside him was a purple crystal and clipboard.

I immediately smelt danger and walked right on by. If only you, Brian, had done the same. But no. Penny Brohn has charged you to become inquisitive and embrace all of life's experiences, and on this Sunday afternoon, Rattle Man was your latest find.

'Are you selling something?' you enquired.

'Hello.' The Rattle Man beamed.

I groaned. Rattle Man had you, and therefore me, in his grasp.

We learnt that when he's not in a health-food shop, he performs Drum Journeys. For the bargain price of £12 an hour, he will drum to you in a local church hall.

'You beat a drum for an hour? I asked. 'Is there anything else?'

'It's really just the drum but sometimes I use the rattle too,' he said, whipping out, from within his knitted rucksack, a box of dried peas on a stick. 'Would you like me to rattle cleanse you here?' he asked.

# FROM ME, TO YOU

There was no way I was getting caught up in a rattle cleanse but you, Brian, you put down your shopping, nodded and stepped into the rattle zone.

Just so passing shoppers wouldn't think this was anything to do with me, I inched further away, clutching my bean sprouts and carton of rice milk.

But Rattle Man had other plans.

'Step closer,' he said. 'I'll rattle cleanse you both together.'

As I huddled in closer, being careful not to catch your eye, Rattle Man crouched on the floor and started to shake his dried-pea box by our feet.

A shudder of laughter rumbled in my stomach.

'Don't laugh, don't laugh,' I told myself. 'It's rude. Don't laugh. Don't look at Brian, don't look at Brian.'

But the laughter bubbled up inside me, rising to my chest as the rattling reached our thighs

'I can't laugh. Oh God, don't let me laugh. Please don't let me laugh.'

I focused on a freezer packed with vegan margarita pizzas.

'Margarita pizza, margarita pizza, margarita pizza,' I chanted. 'Focus on the vegan cheese and forget you now have a rattle being shaken round your waist. Think pizza. Think vegan cheese. Think tomato.'

But all the pizza in the world couldn't save me. The laugh reached my throat and burst out of my mouth. Tears streamed down my face.

Rattle Man was by now up by our chests, the shake more frenzied with every sweep of his hand.

'I've never rattle cleansed someone while they've held their shopping,' he commented.

Another bout of laughter swept through me.

'I'm sorry,' I said. 'I'm not laughing at you, I'm...' But I couldn't get the words out as more tears began to stream down my cheeks.

Of course, I wasn't laughing at him. I was laughing at us, Brian, and how ridiculous we must have looked, standing there as if we were two normal shoppers. On a Sunday afternoon. Being rattle cleansed.

Finally, and thankfully, it ended. You gave him your name and e-mail address and told him you hoped to see him soon on one of his drum journeys.

We paid for our shopping, walked out into the street and collapsed into fits of belly laughter. You swore the rattling had caused The Bag to gurgle and I said the last time I'd been that embarrassed in a shop, I'd been swivelling a hula hoop.

It came as even more of a surprise when you said you were pleased you'd decided not to go straight home from Penny Brohn. Quite frankly, if I was you, I'd be tempted never to visit Chiswick again! But each to their own, Brian.

Much love

Alison

**6 September 2011 – Heatherwood Hospital, Ascot**

Massive day today – scans: CT and MRI. I'd forgotten how bloody noisy those scanning machines are. I could hardly hear my Sounds of the 70s CD.

Felt like I was in a washing machine. Clanging. Vibrating. Whirring. I practised my special Penny Brohn breathing. In. Out. In. Out. Didn't seem to help so I repeated my mantra instead. Cancer gone. Cancer gone. Cancer gone.

Last song on the CD was ABBA's 'Mamma Mia'. One of my mam's favourites.

Wonder what she would have made of all this?

**10 September 2011**

I've been waking up these last few days unable to catch my breath. By today I couldn't bear it any longer so I called the oncologist for scan results. His secretary said he'd call back. Stayed in all day. He called at 5. Swear he must have been able to hear my heart down the phone.

I screamed. Neil rushed in thinking it was bad news. He started to cry with me and then Colin jumped on us. We had a family hug. The Bag is history! Oh yes, and so is the cancer.

# CHAPTER FIFTEEN

## ISN'T NED A DONKEY?

**12 Sept 2011**

Dear Brian

I keep re-reading your text – no, not the one about your all-clear (makes me tearful, in a happy way, but tears and mascara don't mix) but the one about Rattle Man emailing to ask if you would like a private rattle cleanse! Can't believe you pulled in a health food shop!

But coming back to your all-clear, I can't imagine how you must be feeling. It is the most wonderful, wonderful news and I'm so happy for you. In celebration, I will share with you a story of a man rather less fortunate. This morning, I sat in a café, and as I do so often now, had pen hovering over my notebook, desperately trying to catch conversations. At the neighbouring table were a mother, father and two teenage daughters. Two giant jacket potatoes and a sandwich had just been delivered to the table.

'Your soup is on its way,' the waiter told the father.

A minute later, the waiter trotted out of the kitchen with the father's steaming bowl of soup, but en route lost his balance, tripped and the piping hot soup shot onto the father's lap. The man leapt out of his seat, ran into the middle of the café, pulled down his trousers and squealed like a girl.

'Get yourself into the toilet,' the man's wife shouted, embarrassment greater than concern.

'I can't even walk, June, let alone get myself into the toilet,' he snapped, but then he did manage to waddle to the toilet, trousers round his knees.

For the next 15 minutes, he hid himself away. I'd organized ice in a tea towel (you'll remember I had my own burnt flesh experience in a The Mickey Café in EuroDisney, so I'm quite the expert in a hot liquid crisis) and the wife kept vigil at the door, occasionally popping her head round the door, asking, 'More ice?'

Finally, the man emerged, trousers back up. He complained his thumb was burnt and he needed cream.

A burnt thumb?

'Goodness, sir, burnt your thumb?' said the concerned café owner. 'I am sorry. I was going to just knock your meal off the bill but if it's your thumb you've burnt, everything's on me. All your meals are free. More ice for your thumb, perhaps, sir?'

You see, Brian, not everyone is having a good day!

Must go now as I have many chores to do. My washing machine has broken, there's a crack in the bathroom window, and the thermostat doesn't seem to work on the oven. These are tasks for which I have no skills, but worse than that, they are tasks that Tea Taster has no skills for either. One has to start questioning how useful a boyfriend is when he can't do your DIY, however many cups of tea he makes! I bet Neil is a whizz with a screwdriver and a fuse box.

Speak soon, Brian

Much love

Alison

## 12 September 2011

Neil has been secretly liaising with the neighbours and at 7 o'clock tonight I found myself in the middle of my own celebratory dinner. I've never had a surprise party before. Of course, I cried.

We had a lovely evening but I felt removed, like I was watching a movie with me in the starring role. What the hell do I do now? For the last 15 months all I've thought about is this day and now it's here and...

So I had a glass of wine. What the heck!

## 13 September 2011

An almighty hangover! Two glasses of wine! Bloody cancer! Hang on, I can't blame that anymore. I'm clear!

## 17 September 2011

Letter from my oncologist today:

'I am very sorry...'

My stomach fell. Scan results wrong? Mixed me up with someone else? Not clear?

'...that you have had to wait so long for your CT scan results to be confirmed in writing. It is a completely normal scan with no evidence of disease in the bowel or anywhere else in the body.'

Bloody hell!

### 18 September 2011

I am dwelling on yesterday's letter. What if it had been bad news? I should be over the moon but instead I cried. Life is fragile.

### 21 September 2011 – North Hampshire Hospital, Basingstoke

Pre-op assessment today ahead of the big reversal op, or as I'm calling it, The Bag's Funeral. I bumped into 2 of the nurses from last year's hospital stay. They remarked how well I looked. Alison has always said chemo agrees with me.

Shook hands with the junior doctor like he was a long-lost friend, until he said he 'hoped' they'd be able to do reversal. Hope?

Apparently in some cases scar tissue prevents a join. No effing way was I doing any 'hope', The Bag is history. It will happen and it will be the best bit of stitching that doctor has ever done.

### 22 September 2011

Very pleased with my new-found reiki healer, Ron. Penny Brohn was right: I feel energized, and hopefully there's some good being done to my immune system too. I am at least doing my bit to eradicate the need for 'hope'.

I have my bag packed with newly purchased pyjamas and letter from Alison. Wonder if she will carry on writing once The Bag and cancer are gone? I hope so. The letters have created a friendship I never expected but very much enjoy.

**24 September 2011**

Hi Brian

Yesterday I received your text saying you'd had a day feeling sorry for yourself. What weird, complex beings we are. One day you're on top of the world – you've beaten cancer, have a marvellously supportive partner and are all set to start the next phase of your life – and the next day you're in the depths of despair. I say you're entitled to your day of self-pity. Over the last 18 months your life has been turned upside down, and 'all-clear' you may be, but the C-word still hovers around, waiting to scare you at your next scan. Revel in your misery days because they are a reminder you're still alive. Look them in the face and laugh as you challenge them to do their worst because you know you only have to go to bed and wait for the next day to begin to be one step closer back to joy.

And as the sole purpose of my letters is to make you smile, then here is today's chuckle. It has been a while since Tea Taster wished me Happy

# FROM ME, TO YOU

Christmas on Easter Sunday, put his watch back rather than forwards at the last hour change, or asked if Steve Jobs' biography had a happy ending, so I knew it was time for a Tea Taster 'special'.

Last Sunday, at a family christening, Tea Taster and his cousins were deliberating how Alfie, Tea Taster's middle child, had come to be so tall. Tea Taster tried to claim it was from him.

'But you're not even six foot, are you?' pointed out one of the cousins. (Of course, in Tea Taster's world, everyone is young, tall and dashing – most of all himself).

Each family member, past and present, recounted stories, trying to identify the carrier of the tall gene. Finally, they remembered great uncle Bill. Great uncle Bill, 6'4", had been a prisoner of war in Japan. Each cousin had a tale of how terribly uncle Bill been treated and how, for the rest of his life, he hated anything to do with Japan and the Japanese.

'He never did get over his time in Japan,' said one cousin. 'Once, he came to stay with us but at the airport he refused to get in the car. It was a Toyota Corolla.'

After a moment's thought, Tea Taster nodded and said, 'Well, he was very tall and they are such small cars. I can understand that.'

And now to finish off, here are some overheard conversations from my notebook of joy:

A teenage boy, and what appeared to be his grandmother, were sitting in a café, both reading the menu.

'What are you having?' the woman asked, nudging the boy's arm.

'Dunno,' he replied, moving his arm away from her reach.

'What do you think I should have?' she asked. 'I'm a bit limited. I've forgotten to put my bottom teeth in.'

The boy dropped his head, moved his chair a little further away and muttered, 'Soup?'

'Mmmm,' she said. 'Do you think I could risk a macaroni cheese?'

Overheard in a charity shop: 'I used to collect white China but then I had a hysterectomy.'

Two old, but very elegant, ladies, probably in their eighties, were on the train chatting about hair and make-up:

'I'm thinking of getting my eyebrows tattooed on,' said one, skimming her finger lightly along the perfect line of her brow. 'I'm fed up of pencilling them on.'

'Aren't you afraid that they might rub off?' asked the other, whose own eyebrows were dark, perfectly shaped and clearly needed no pencilling.

The first woman shook her head. 'Tattoos don't rub off.'

'Not even in the swimming pool?' asked her friend.

'Oh, do you think? The chlorine? I'll have to ask the beautician.'

'Or just don't put your head under the water.'

My new interest is flash fiction – it seems these are stories that are very very short. I wonder if any of my anecdotes are flash fiction. Apparently, they have competitions. For short stories. Who knew?

Am off now, Brian. I hope my letter has made you smile in the midst of your doldrums and that they pass as quickly as they came.

Much love

Alison

**28 September 2011 – North Hampshire Hospital, Basingstoke**

The waiting room is full. There are some nice dressing gowns in here, I notice, but none as smart as my new, swanky one from M&S,

especially purchased for this momentous day. I wonder if all these men are having a bag removed? How many of them have been told they're cancer free? I'm looking forward to the anaesthetic – slipping away into oblivion.

Think I just saw someone admiring my dressing gown.

### 29 September 2011 – North Hampshire Hospital, Basingstoke

I woke up 5 hours ago. Felt my tummy. There was a bag shaped lump. The nurse must have seen my expression because she smiled and said, 'Everything went well. It's gone.'

I could have leapt out of bed and kissed her.

It's gone. It's all gone.

### 30 September 2011 – North Hampshire Hospital, Basingstoke

Strange night as my bowel wakes up after ten months of rest. Seems it has forgotten how to work. That and the fact it is now minus a rectum. Spent much of the night on the loo. Thankfully, Sudocrem is not just for babies' bums. Instant relief.

### 4 October 2011 – North Hampshire Hospital, Basingstoke

I can go home – brilliant. Although how the hell I am going to get there without having an accident, I don't know. So far today: 25 trips to the loo.

Dietician called in to say hello and said that I can now eat anything and everything. Farewell food list; hello more toilet visits.

## 6 October 2011

I have been pondering the rectum, now that I don't have one. I've learnt the importance of the rectum, and why I'm now on a constant trip to and from the toilet. When the colon fills up, stool passes into the rectum which sends messages to the brain to move the bowels. Infants and babies don't have the muscle control to delay this movement, hence pooing their pants. I no longer have a rectum, hence pooing my pants.

## 9 October 2011

Hi Brian

I hadn't planned to send a letter so soon. After all, I only spoke to you last night. But I sensed you were not feeling quite as elated as you imagined you would. Remember, it is only a short time since your operation and the most gruelling year your body has ever experienced.

Do you recall the photograph you took outside the radiotherapy department on the first day of your treatment? All relaxed and smiling. It was almost as if you were going on an adventure. And now that adventure is almost over. That in itself must be daunting. So, when you sit there feeling frustrated and uncertain, don't be hard on yourself. It will be the small steps that get you to the next stage (not to the end - as we know that in the cycle of life's clouds and sunshine, there is no end to a journey, but just to the next place you are meant to be).

And speaking of the next place, now you're well again, I guess our corresponding days will soon be drawing to a close. I did only offer to write till you were better. My letters have become a lovely part of my life but maybe if they are no longer needed, I'll be kick-started into doing something else with my writing. However, I'm not going to dwell on this, as it makes me sad to think I may not be writing to you in the near future. And how can I possibly be sad when the reason I won't be writing is because you are CLEAR?

Much love

Alison

**9 October 2011**

So tired. Seems waking every 2 hours for the loo is my new norm. For a minute, I wished The Bag back. At least I could leave the house. It will get better, won't it? Perhaps thinking I can eat anything and everything may be a little premature.

**11 October 2011**

I made it to Waitrose this morning. Treated myself to some Tena Men. Much as I marvel at the existence of such things, with their 'boosted absorption, odour control and masculine and discreet fit', I still looked over my shoulder as I shoved them under the bag of potatoes in my basket. And I made sure I used the self-service checkout.

Colin let me pick him up this afternoon. He must have got used to my new smell.

**18 October 2011**

Booked tickets for London Gay Men's Chorus Christmas concert. Something to look forward to. And this makes up for missing it last year. I'm going to make this an annual Christmas event.

**24 October 2011**

Down to less than 10 times to the loo today. Dietary changes have helped.

Food list back up and running:

> Seeds – no
>
> Nuts – no
>
> Banana – no
>
> Yoghurt – God no

But I am now taking Colin for walks and my Tena Men are preventing any embarrassments. But God, my bum is so sore!

**28 October 2011**

I have forgotten how to make decisions. No diary of hospital appointments, treatment schedules, playing the C-card when I want to get out of something. No one telling me what to do, or where to be. I feel lost.

Only 8 times to the loo today and once in the night.

**4 November 2011**

I feel very wary about the future. Things are supposed to move back to normal but I don't know what that is. I am not the same as I was before diagnosis. I've been sick for over a year and my life has been governed by the cancer and its greed for appointments and treatment.

But, it is time to be brave. I need to find something else to fill my time. But what the hell might that be? It's all very well me trying to help Alison find her passion, but what the hell is mine? What do I know how to do that's not life on a commuter train?

**9 November 2011**

A lovely surprise in the post today – a postcard from Alison with her latest overheard conversation.

*The mother in the café was flicking through a magazine, her young son fidgeting by her side.*

*'What are they doing?' he asked, pointing at the opened page.*

*'It's an advert for a spa,' she replied. 'He's having a massage.'*

*The boy slurped the last of his milkshake.*

*'Can you get massages all over your body?' he asked.*

*'Yes,' she said. 'Legs, back, chest.'*

*'Do they do your ding dong?'*

*The mother blushed but managed to keep a straight face.*

*'Well, that's a different kind of massage,' she replied.*

*'So they do do it. That's good.'*

## 15 November 2011

I sent an email to PwC, thanked them for their patience but said I have decided not to go back. Decision made. All thanks to Alison's strategy day, getting me to think about careers, passions and the passing of every day.

Turned out not to be the only decision of the day – I joined the gym. Walking Colin is not enough to rebuild my strength and stamina. From next week, I will be at the gym 2 mornings a week. The endorphins will help get me through these dark, winter days.

6 times to the loo today.

## 18 November 2011

The food list is working well – not too many veggies or fruit. Little and often seems to be the way forward. I have also lost a few pounds but not surprising as nothing hangs around for long. Might buy shares in Andrex.

## 22 November 2011

Leftover bags delivered to Colostomy UK today. They're off to a good home in Africa as the NHS can't take them back. I have never even contemplated that people in Africa have stoma bags. I kept one as a reminder and put it in a Paul Smith bag in the drawer. I'm sure he won't mind.

## 23 November 2011

Rosemary called in last night to discuss a dating dilemma. Her new man does not fit any of her usual criteria. In her words, he is not handsome but instead an ex-rugby player with a broken nose, a cauliflower ear and is bald. And short. But he makes her laugh. Neil pointed out it was my sense of humour that attracted him to me. Bit shocked to discover it wasn't my looks!

## 25 November 2011

Still not been to the gym. Seems making the decisions are only half the task!

### 26 November 2011 – Fitness First, Camberley

Took a deep breath and braved the gym, and pleased I did. I got 3 complimentary personal training sessions to get me on track. Was dreading a 'bottom incident' but it behaved, which, with all the lifting and stretching I was doing, was an achievement. I've booked a personal trainer session for next week.

### 29 November 2011 – Wexham Park Hospital, Slough

Co-rectal cancer nurse was very impressed with my progress and said it took some patients a year to get to where I now am. Felt pleased – I'm on a par with a toddler being potty trained apparently. High fives all round!

### 30 November 2011 – Fitness First, Camberley

Personal trainer Steve is very patient. He's reassured me I am not the least fit client he has ever had and, considering my health over the last 12 months, I'm doing very well. Charmer! I even broke into sweat on the treadmill. What I hadn't anticipated was how mentally great the training would make me feel. I feel very positive, have not needed my usual afternoon nap and my bum is behaving.

### 8 December 2011

Another decision made today – sorted out my wardrobe. Monty Don is on his way to the charity shop and slim-fitting Diesel jeans are back. Knew there'd be some benefit to all this toilet activity as I now need a belt. My bum looks rather good in these jeans – must be all that buttock clenching.

**16 December 2011**

Hi Brian

As we haven't actually had a conversation to agree I'll stop writing now you're better, I thought I'd round off the year with one last missive. In the new year, I'm expecting all my writing talents to be taken up with works of fiction, but more on that later.

I can't believe we are almost done with 2011 (and my letters) – what a lot has been crammed in. Well, a lot for you. Mine has been eventful but I'm not sure I'm any further on than when I first began writing. However, if someone should stop me in the street for market research purposes (or part of a survey for a trashy magazine) and ask my greatest achievement of 2011, I shall answer that I wrote letters to my friend Brian and now he's cured of cancer. Won't be my fault if they assume the two are connected and ask for a double page spread. It'll be better than saying I achieved nothing in 2011. Although, perhaps Brené Brown would disagree. Have you watched her Ted Talk? It's quite the sensation of the moment. Basically, she says, with much humour and warmth, that society is split into two kinds of people: those who feel worthy of being loved and those who don't. And the commonality between those in the former group is that they dare to be vulnerable. They are not ashamed. She goes on to say that once we allow ourselves to be vulnerable, then we connect with others and those connections are the life blood of our souls. And we are happy. That's big, isn't it?

I had never imagined that by allowing ourselves to be more vulnerable we would be happier. And of course, there are a plethora of books that tell us that if we're happy we stand a better chance of being healthy and fighting illness.

Recently, I received a letter from my godmother. She wrote:

'I was beginning to feel a bit down lately because my working days are over. Needing a change of scene, I went to my local shopping mall and had the obligatory cup of coffee. The lady at the next table looked a bit down, so I struck up a conversation. She told me she had breast cancer and her treatment had resulted in her losing her hair (strangely, I had commented on how nice her hair looked – it was a wig). She said she had never opened up to anyone before about her cancer but felt she could with me. How wonderful to be, in some small way, a prop for this lady. And I have to say too, the wigs available nowadays are really super.'

I smiled when I read this but, in writing it here, I realise when one person shows us their vulnerability, they not only give themselves a boost of worthiness, they give one to the person they've opened up to as well.

So, in the spirit of vulnerability, I've booked myself onto an Arvon residential writing course for a week in January. No doubt I will be the dunce of the class but hey ho, I'm all about the vulnerability now. And it means I can ignore the fact that in a whole 18 months I haven't found my next career.

I also have other news but it's not for a letter. Please, you and Neil, come to supper on the 23rd.

Much love

Alison

## 16 December 2011

Cutting Edge Basingstoke want me to have a colonoscopy. Nothing to worry about, they say. Last one was a year ago so best to do another. Hoping it will be after Christmas as the thought of taking that Picolax to clear my insides out makes me feel nauseous.

No blood test results yet – no news is good news, yes?

## 17 December 2011 – Cadogan Hall, London

Loved the London Gay Men's Chorus Christmas concert. We had great seats and I got quite taken away by the music, even crying at Wham's 'Last Christmas' – it reminded me of how ill I was a year ago and how grateful I am to still be here. Neil's face was a picture throughout – he loves a good Christmas tune. I love that man for being with me over the last 12 months. I am so lucky. When they sang 'Perfect Year', I whispered to him that 2012 will be the perfect year. And it will.

## 22 December 2011 – North Hampshire Hospital, Basingstoke

Colonoscopy is all clear – no polyps, nothing. Phew. Bring on Christmas! I am loving Radio 2's selection of cheesy Christmas songs.

I can eat anything this year without worrying whether The Bag will explode but still pleased we're doing Christmas at home in case I need the loo after too much champagne.

## 23 December 2011 – Alison's flat

Pre-Christmas dinner with Alison and Tea Taster at her flat. A year ago we weren't close enough friends to even think about doing this. Didn't mention the letters potentially stopping. She's busy now with Tea Taster, her trips to Dorset and kids to look after (however much she 'kids' herself) – not sure she'll have time for letters anyway. I will really miss them. And I will miss her. But best news of the evening – her and Tea Taster are engaged. We all drank champagne and, of course, I cried.

# CHAPTER SIXTEEN

## NEED A NEW JOURNAL FOR NEW BEGINNINGS

**1 January 2012**

Hi Brian

I am writing a letter to prove to myself I can still actually write. I am afflicted; I have writer's block. This is a disaster – just days before my residential writing course where I've been asked to rock up with a piece of my own prose. For the last 18 months, the words have flowed. But no more. Just at the time I need to be at my most creative, I am stumped into writing silence. And to make it worse – if it could get any worse – I've heard that on the final evening you read out your work to the group. Oh God. I'm not going. What was I doing thinking I could be a writer anyway? I'm staying at home. Forget all that vulnerability rubbish.

On second thoughts, time away will mean I can escape my flat, and more specifically, the kitchen. Over the last month, the kitchen has turned against me. We've never had the best relationship – I ignore it for weeks and, when I do pay it some attention, it's usually only to take a bottle of wine out of the fridge. However, this week the kitchen has sought revenge. The washing machine irreparably broke but the new one won't sit flush due to a previously unknown, weird curve of the wall behind. The installation of the new washing machine has upset the dishwasher and so its door now won't close and this, in turn, has caused the plinth to loosen, and every now and again it falls forward, to reveal what I can only think are rat poison pellets.

And then today, as if all this wasn't enough, I opened the freezer to take out one of your delicious, home-made mince pies, to be faced with a solid layer of ice. I don't even know why I bother with a freezer; it seems so excessive just for ice cubes. So, I now need to defrost it. I think I'm supposed to do something with a hairdryer but won't that just result in a puddle of water, which I'll then have to clear up? The only saving grace I can see is that once your mince pies are defrosted, I shall be forced to eat them all.

All this talk of ice reminds me of Tea Taster's comment to my sister recently, just as they stepped onto a festive outdoor ice rink.

'Jane, I must tell you something,' he said, holding on to her arm. 'When you get on the ice, it will be terribly slippery.'

I am engaged to a very profound man!

Brian, by the time you get this letter, it is unlikely I'll be on my kitchen floor electrocuted by my own hair dryer, but will instead be in the Shropshire countryside with the other would-be writers. Wish me luck. I can't think anyone is going to take me seriously as a writer when all I've done is write letters to you but...

Much love

Alison

**7 January 2012**

Searched internet all day for my dream beach house with ocean view. A celebratory holiday. South Africa here we come. This time, cancer won't scupper us. And Alison has much to celebrate too - off on a writing course with a diamond on her finger. 2012 already off to a perfect start.

**8 January 2012**

Call from consultant at Cutting Edge Basingstoke. Biopsy all clear; I'd forgotten they'd even done one. But CEA levels in blood test are high so he's arranging a CT scan. Might be a blip, he said. Trying to distract myself with endless internet searches for all things South Africa.

What will I tell Neil when he gets home?

**9 January 2012**

A letter arrived, but not from Alison. From Cutting Edge. No point keeping this one to open later with a cup of tea. Scan is 13th January 3.00pm. It mentioned slightly raised blood levels. That's promising. Probably just inflammation.

**10 January 2012 – Fitness First, Camberley**

I just had the best PT session. Interval training. Lifting weights. Stretching. Endorphins a go go! I feel so energised and alive. Clearly not ill.

# FROM ME, TO YOU

**11 Jan 2012**

Dear Brian

I'm sorry if this letter is scrawly but I'm on the plane back from Ireland and the turbulence has us all bouncing around like corks in the sea. I wanted to write while I was over there but time got away. I'll explain Ireland in a moment – what I really want to tell you about is the writing course.

I loved it, loved it, loved it! The words flowed, I didn't want each day to end and couldn't wait for the next to begin. And can you believe, the toilet in my bedroom was sponsored by Maggie Smith? Felt like I was on a throne every time I went for a pee.

I told them all about you, that you are my muse, that there'd have been no words without you and, should I ever write a novel, I shall be dedicating it to, 'My great friend Brian and his cancer – without the two, pen would never have touched paper.'

What I did learn was if I really do want to be a writer then I need to write every day, collect ideas and observe people. Then turn these all into believable characters and thrilling plotlines. So, my notebook is going to be working overtime.

But why am I on a plane from Ireland?

I had a call last week from an ex-colleague. Did I fancy doing a bit of consultancy work? And, as we said at our strategy day, with the art auction done, I do need something to do. So, I dusted off my 'knock 'em dead, you power-woman' dress and got on a plane to Ireland for an interview.

Tom, the taxi driver, will be at the airport to meet you, my colleague had promised. Look out for your name on his board. In Arrivals, there was no board, so I waited. Other passengers paired up with taxi drivers but I was left unclaimed. Finally, there were just two of us left: me and a man who'd been standing there all that time.

'Is it Alison?' he asked as he walked towards me.

'Yes. You're not Tom the taxi driver, are you?'

'I am, to be sure. I knew we'd recognise each other. Welcome to Ireland.'

Of course, Tom has gone straight in the notebook and awaits the life of a short story to be breathed into him. That's if I have time to write – I got the contract and I'm back in Ireland next week, when Tom and I may well indeed recognise one another again.

Fear not, Brian, I'm not slipping back into the corporate world. I'm just doing someone a favour for a couple of weeks. I know I have to find my passion.

Much love

Alison

**11 January 2012**

Holiday booked with absolutely no expense spared. Told Neil there's no way we're scrimping on this one. I deserve this but so does he. It's my thank you to him. Beautiful villa overlooking the ocean, infinity pool, a bathroom each. Perfect.

**12 January 2012**

Whose smart idea was it to see War Horse? Am sitting here at 4am still sobbing. I've woken up because I can't stop dreaming about that poor animal. One bad thing after another and still he carried on.

Scan tomorrow so need to go back to bed and sleep.

## 13 January 2012 – North Hampshire Hospital, Basingstoke

The scan was just a scan – nothing unusual. Just the same old same old.

But now I'm tired.

## 14 January 2012

I hate the radio. The song lyrics are sending out messages.

Hearts breaking. Missing loved ones. Being strong.

How will it be for Neil if I'm not here?

Oh, for goodness sake, it was only 18 months ago I didn't think he should stay. When will I learn? I am not responsible for other people's lives. Seems I have a God complex!

## 15 January 2012

Got confirmation on beach villa reservation.

Wasn't as excited as I thought I would be.

## 16 January 2012

Cutting Edge called. Appointment to see consultant in 3 days. They don't fit you in that quickly for no reason.

Rushed to get off the phone as I struggled to breathe. Or stand. Colin ran over, thinking I was kneeling down to play. But then he placed his paw on my arm. He's never done that before. He knew.

**16 Jan 2012**

Hi Brian

Sorry not to have been able to call in to see you as I drove down the M3 this last weekend on my way to Dorset. I hope everything is OK.

Before I left London, I spoke to my mum, who was on the coffee and biscuit break midway through her Tai Chi class. She said she wished me luck with the Hitchcock family weekend, to which I told her it wasn't necessary as Tea Taster is very much in charge and in control of everything family.

'I'm doing slow-roast pork,' Tea Taster declared on Saturday morning. 'And we'll pick at it all weekend. It will be delicious. It's a celebration for Billy.'

Saturday was due to be a big day for 11-year-old Billy - his first Taekwondo belt grading. In the excitement of the slow-roast pork, Tea Taster had forgotten that I'm a vegetarian, that on the weekends Alfie only eats Subways and because Billy is reading Anne Frank's Diary, he had declared himself Jewish the previous day.

Of course, Tea Taster had no idea how to cook a slow-roast so whipped out a few cookbooks. Every food writer recommended roasting the pork for between 8 and 24 hours, 8 being the absolute minimum. As we were going to be out for the day, with no idea how long we'd be at the belt-grading, Tea Taster um'd and ah'd as to whether to put the pork in before we left. He decided against it, confident that we'd only be out for a few hours.

Eight long hours later we drudged back into the house. It turns out that belt gradings go in no particular order. Billy's three-minute grading happened at the end of the day - a day of no internet connection, of a café serving only KitKats and stewed tea, and of us never daring to leave the hall just in case Billy was next.

Two hours after returning home, Billy and I were hungry and wondering when our celebration meal would be on the table. Tea Taster bumbled around and mumbled for a while, opening and closing the oven door, before declaring that he'd have to speed up the cooking process.

# FROM ME, TO YOU

'I'll whack up the heat.'

And so, at 7.30pm, we sat down to a rather fast (and tasteless) slow roast pork. Even Lizzie was reluctant to bother with scraps, taking a pitiful sniff before returning to her basket.

A forlorn Tea Taster, conscious of our disappointment and in a bid to lift spirits, promised a 'Taekwondo Surprise' for dessert.

Triumphantly, he brought to the table three meringue nests piled high with strawberries and cream.

'You know I don't like meringues,' said Billy.

'And I'm allergic to strawberries,' I joined in.

Poor Tea Taster's face fell. We had, between us, right royally pissed all over his celebrations. But Billy had a silver lining.

'Alison,' he said, crumbling his meringue on the floor for Lizzie. 'When you're married to Dad and live with us, you'll be doing the cooking, won't you?'

I swear Lizzie laughed. As will my mum when I tell her. But I don't mind them laughing, Brian. And if this letter has made you laugh — that's all that matters really.

Much love

Alison

**17 January 2012**

Spoke to Alison today. Seems she's as much in Dorset as she's in London these days but all she wanted to talk about was her writing course. I expect her letters will improve now – that is if she doesn't get distracted and start writing stories. I hope she doesn't forget me. I may need her.

Felt like a complete damp squib telling her my fears about the cancer. I haven't spoken to anyone except Neil but I wanted to talk to her. Maybe I hoped that some of her newfound enthusiasm for life would rub off on me. She listened but didn't ask the 1 question I didn't want to answer: if the cancer is back, will it still be in my bowel or have moved elsewhere?

**18 January 2012**

Today I am an ostrich. If I don't go to the hospital appointment, I can just carry on as normal and go on holiday. Deal with it when I get back. I suggest this to Neil. Goes down like cold sick.

**19 January 2012 – North Hampshire Hospital, Basingstoke**

Sitting in the waiting room, I had that weird feeling, the one where you almost step off the kerb in front of an oncoming car.

The consultant smiled as he invited us into his office. I thought the buzzing sound must be the heater but when Neil tapped my arm, I realised it was my breathing. I looked at the nurse for a clue. Nothing.

'2-3 cm tumour on the liver', 'rogue cell escaped the chemo', 'metastasized to your liver'... I heard, but it was like I wasn't in the room. I'd stepped off the kerb.

I looked at Neil to save me. His face was white. The nurse looked sad.

The consultant explained the tumour could be cut out and the liver would regrow. All that's needed is a referral to another consultant.

Really? That simple?

Neil and I didn't speak or look at each other as we crossed the car park. Once in the car, I howled. Grief. Disappointment. Injustice. Anger. I howled and howled. And then howled some more, until my head hurt, my chest hurt, my heart hurt. Neil tried to hold me but I couldn't bear to be touched. He rested his hand on mine, his body shaking with sobs. Eventually we calmed.

I have let us down. I can't beat cancer. All that positive thinking, visualising – pointless! Cancer is back and it's raging through our life again. I have let everyone down. I am a failure.

# CHAPTER SEVENTEEN

## NEW JOURNAL ON HOLD

**20 January 2012**

I wait for Neil to go to work and then google Stage IV cancer. I want stories of people who have survived. Instead, I get this:

*There is usually no cure for Stage IV cancer and due to it having spread throughout the body it is unlikely it can be completely removed. The goal of treatment is to prolong survival and improve quality of life.*

I don't google survival rates – I don't need to; I know they're shit. I've never been in the top percentage of anything so no reason I will be with cancer. I never attained the top grades at school, never one of the kids picked for the football team, didn't get a 1st at Uni, not even many matches on Grindr.

Spent rest of the morning googling hospices.

**24 January 2012**

Reiki yesterday. It had been booked weeks ago so the timing was meant to be. I lie on the couch, looked up Ron's nose and told him everything. He said he would be focusing the healing on my chakra points – not a phrase I've heard since yoga in India.

I expected nothing but felt a very warm positive sensation on my right side, close to my abdomen.

And then the tears flowed. No sounds. No fear. Just sadness. Streams of calm tears.

Last night I slept well. No dreams.

**24 Jan 2012**

Hi Brian

Am hoping this gets to you before you set off on holiday – something to entertain you on the plane. I know you will tell me the results of your scan in your own time. I am taking no news as good news.

The 'Hitchcocks Visit London' weekend has drawn to a close and I can, once again, breathe, reclaim my flat and, therapeutically, recount it in a letter. It had seemed like a good idea when first planned – Alfie was in London on work experience, so Tea Taster and Billy would come up for the weekend and Alfie would make his way over to mine on the Friday night. What could be nicer?

(And just as an aside, I thought I'd try to write this in the style of a story to practice some of the stuff I learnt on my writing course.)

'What time they arriving?' grunted Alfie as he walked into the living room, the smell of Pot Noodle wafting before him. He'd only arrived half an hour ago and already the flat stunk. 'And Billy's not sleeping in the same bed as me, is he?'

It was seven o'clock and I was enjoying the last moments of peace before Tea Taster and Billy arrived, hopefully with the blow-up bed.

The doorbell rang. Alfie jumped up, unable to disguise his excitement.

'I'll let them in.'

Noises of hugging back slaps followed.

'You brought my Xbox with you?' he enquired before Tea Taster had even stepped into the hallway. 'I need it.'

They congregated in the living room, complete with a blow-up bed, overnight bags, bottle of wine, Xbox and a bunch of daffodils.

Billy danced around the space.

'Alfie, Alfie, do you want to see my Taekwondo? I passed yellow belt grading last week.'

Alfie ignored him.

Tea Taster disappeared into the kitchen.

'I brought lovely flowers,' he called back. 'I'll put them in a vase.'

Alfie moved his Xbox to the bedroom, away from Billy's flailing Taekwondo limbs, and returned with a skateboard.

'Dad,' he shouted. 'Come look at my new deck. It's so neat. It's a seven and a half. Bought it with my work experience money.'

Tea Taster darted into the room, bunch of daffodils in hand. Of course, he had no more idea about a seven and a half than I did but he cooed at the board, cradling it as if it were a baby.

'I've been doing double spins,' boasted Alfie. 'Cool as biscuits.'

Billy continued his Taekwondo whirling dervish routine as Alfie skated down the hallway.

'Look, Alfie, this is the move I learned last night.'

Alfie ignored him.

'Oh yeah, and Dad, I've got you some Goose.' Alfie darted into the room and returned with three bottles of Grey Goose vodka. He handed one to Tea Taster.

Alfie's work experience had been as a pot-washer for his uncle's mixology business, and over the course of the week he had come to learn the value of The Goose.

'Last night, we did this celebrity party,' Alfie said. 'It was some bloke who has a theatre in London. I dunno. Kev or Cam or something. Anyway, I got these three bottles for doing an extra hour, which is well sweet as they're worth like £20 each and I only get paid £7.50 an hour.'

I asked if he intended to sell them to recoup the cash but he said they were too valuable to sell and instead he'd be taking them to Lance's party next month.

'Imagine how cool I'm going to look when I walk in with these,' he said, one bottle in each hand, arms draped as if escorting two blonde beauties. 'Sweeeeeet.'

Tea Taster nodded and returned to the kitchen to arrange his daffodils.

'While you're in there, can you cook me some dinner? I was going to have packet rice,' Alfie shouted.

'Sure.' Tea Taster delighted to be able to mother his son again.

Billy was still spinning.

'What you doing, gay-boy?' asked Alfie.

Thrilled to have the attention, Billy bowed and began a routine. Alfie joined in, high-kicking towards Billy's head.

'No,' Billy shouted. 'We're not allowed to use our Taekwondo for violence. Mrs Roberts says—'

He didn't get a chance to finish his sentence as Alfie knocked him over with a tap of his foot.

'And,' cried Billy from the floor, 'you can't call me gay-boy 'cos it's a der... dergoraroter... a derog...'

His scramble for the right word ended with a plea to me. I beckoned him over and whispered in his ear.

He turned to Alfie, chest plumped and shouted out my whispered cue, 'A darn good word.'

They both looked at me, puzzled, but Alfie took advantage of the pause and tackled Billy to the floor, tickling him relentlessly until Billy could barely breathe with laughter, his legs kicking out involuntarily.

Suddenly, Alfie shrieked, grabbed his neck and stumbled to a standing position.

'Dad, come quick. I've broke my neck. I can't move,' Alfie cried out, then continued to whine how he was paralysed and it was a nightmare as it meant he wouldn't be able to skate. All the while, Billy continued his taekwondo, with

Lizzie snapping at his heels. Oh yes, I forgot to mention, the dog was with us as well.

Later, Tea Taster fed packet rice to a 'paralysed' Alfie – or he did until Lizzie jumped onto Alfie's knee, causing him to start and jar his neck further, causing the rice to spill all over the floor. At the same time, finally having exhausted his martial arts routines, Billy stood up and burst into song. 'Empty Chairs at Empty Tables' from Les Misérables, this year's school production. He has a good singing voice but is usually crippled with nerves. Desperate to be in the show, at the audition, he'd asked the teachers to stand in the cupboard while he sang. With no visible audience, his nerves disappeared, and he got a part.

'You're so weird,' snapped Alfie, addressing the wall, unable to turn to face Billy.

And so, the evening went on, Billy laughing at Alfie, Alfie snapping at everyone and Tea Taster making cups of tea, arranging daffodils and finally helping Alfie to his room, undressing him and putting him to bed.

And I never moved from the sofa.

(End of story bit. I was never very good at endings in school essays. Seems little has changed.)

Anyway, Bri, that was just the Friday evening. I had two more days to go but perhaps that's a letter for another time. Suffice it to say that, by the end of the weekend, I needed therapy and more than a shot of Goose.

I must sign off now. I have an early start tomorrow as I'm flying back to Ireland (although, compared to being with Family Hitchcock, working in Ireland is a complete doddle). On that note, however, there's other stuff to tell you about Ireland, and I know you're not going to approve, but let's not worry about that now. More Goose anyone?

Much love

Alison

### 30 January 2012 – North Hampshire Hospital, Basingstoke

In spite of all her head-shaking, I can't help but like Miss W – reassuring, knowledgeable and pretty. What else can you wish for in your liver surgeon?

She was shaking her head before I'd even finished telling her I'd be available for surgery after our holiday. There is no way of telling how fast the tumour is growing and it's close to the hepatic vein and if it gets in there then chemo is the only treatment, but it's thought that

I may be chemo resistant, which I know, as I wouldn't be there if I wasn't. Felt as if she was gabbling but she wasn't. I was just propelling her to the inevitable line: 'We need to operate as soon as possible. You'll need to cancel your holiday.'

I smiled over my anger.

This cancer has robbed me of my celebratory holiday – the bastard.

## 31 January 2012

I am at a loss for what to do with myself. I am so angry; I am resorting to weepy DVDs – Bette Midler's Beaches today. It will bring back memories of Caesar's Palace in the BC era. That was 5 years ago.

This is how I view time now: Before Cancer and Cancer. In the C era, I have urges to sob. Loudly. And I do. For some reason, it feels like a good thing to do. In the BC era, I never sobbed.

## 2 February 2012

I am full of self-pity. It's dark and negative. Haven't I been through enough? Just when I was getting back on track. Am even resorting to the visualisation technique I learnt at Penny Brohn. Rolodex of images: shimmering lakes, waves on a beach, sunshine dappling through forest canopies. But I see nothing. For God's sake.

In a passing moment of bliss, I do spot myself shopping in John Lewis. Then I see Monty Don and the bubble bursts.

**3 February 2012**

Neil pointed out I hadn't opened Alison's letter. 'Might cheer you up,' he said.

As ever, it starts with comedy headed notepaper – a goose this time. Always makes me smile.

Wonder what it is she has to tell me, although I think I can guess. She doesn't know I have news for her too.

**6 February 2012**

Passed pre-op assessment with flying colours.

Still can't get my head round having 60% of my liver cut away, nor fact that until a week ago, I couldn't even accurately pinpoint where my liver was.

Reiki Ron tells me that when I am in hospital my guardian angel will be looking over me. Always handy.

**13 February 2012 – North Hampshire Hospital, Basingstoke**

Morphine gets its name from Morpheus – the God of Dreams. My anaesthetist is a mine of interesting medical facts and is entertaining the 4 of us in the ward.

Lovely Miss W and Mr R, the main man in liver surgery, called in to see me. They're both going to be in theatre tomorrow so I will be in their safe hands. I will ring Neil later to tell him not to worry. Even Bert in the corner bed thinks I'm lucky. Mr R is the best in the business, he says. Bert also tells me about his mobility scooter and the No 2 bus timetable – he seems to be an expert in both.

### 14 February 2012 – North Hampshire Hospital, Basingstoke

Operation Liver is upon me. Was up, showered and ready by 6am, like an excited schoolboy. Chatty Bert was awake and munching his cornflakes. He asked if Neil was my boy - I think he meant son rather than boyfriend. The lighting in here must be awful.

I text Gillian and Alison to tell them where I am and apologise that this will be something of a shock as neither of them even know the cancer is back. Managing other people's emotions through my illness is not something I'm getting any better at.

The flutter in my stomach must be down to looking forward to the anaesthetic. I love drifting off into oblivion, escaping the world and having no memory of what happened while you were away. This is not how I expected to feel this morning.

### 16 February 2012 – North Hampshire Hospital, Basingstoke

Finally out of ICU after 24 hours of post-op observation. I am a tangle of wires, tubes, drains and monitors. I'm looked after by Nurse Rashi. We talk about Goa and her kids. She was very sorry to hear I didn't have children. When I told her it wasn't really an option for me and my male partner, she replied with, 'Well it didn't stop Elton John, did it?'

Miss W said everything went according to plan and they've got very good margins from the removal. Mr R dropped by too. Lovely curly hair, I noticed.

Enjoying the morphine pump. Definitely helps with sleeping. Helps with everything to be honest.

**20 February 2012**

Feeling rather smug as I'm home days earlier than expected. Miss W said I'm one of her best patients. Brought back down to earth when I looked at the scar in the mirror. I look like I've been attacked by a shark – a vicious red line down my right side starting just under the ribcage. I didn't linger.

**21 February 2012**

Colin ran away today – from Neil. And he ran straight back home to me. He knows he needs to take care of me. And once again, he works his magic as the rest of the morning's conversation is about runaway Colin rather than about how well my stitches are healing and whether I need more painkillers.

**23 February 2012**

Today I was supposed to be flying to South Africa – but I don't mind being here on the sofa.

# More butter, anyone?

**18 Feb 2012**

Hi Brian

This is your convalescence letter. I was so sorry to receive your text but I'm so glad, and honoured, that you did share your news. Brené Brown would applaud your vulnerability, I'm sure. And in the spirit of friendship and connection, I need to start off with my own news.

I know I said Ireland was just for a couple of weeks but, as luck would have it, they like me, have upped my rate and offered me more work. So, I've said yes, but only while I find something else to do. I am not, I repeat NOT, slipping back into corporate life. I am going to keep on searching for my passion. And at least, this way, by keeping myself busy, I don't intrude too much into Hitchcock family time, even though Ireland is turning out to be just as loopy as the Hitchcocks.

I was required to facilitate a meeting of the Board last time I went. The CEO was very keen for HR Director Niamh to attend this time as she had so far missed out on the beginning of the project due to maternity leave. He said he didn't mind me repeating last time's meeting content and was 99% sure Niamh was in the boardroom already and that everyone would be there by 9.00am. At 9.00 I casually enquired of the group if she was on her way.

The group, looking puzzled, said, 'No, she's not in the office today. She's on maternity leave. She was never due to be in today.'

At that moment the CEO walked in. You're going to look a bit daft now, I thought, as I explained Niamh wasn't there. But no look of surprise crossed his face.

'OK,' he said. 'Let's crack on anyway.'

Let's crack on? I got up at 4.30am, dragged myself onto a plane, met Tom the Taxi Driver (we recognised each other) and the reason for me being there wasn't even in the room. At least I now know why the Irish use the phrase 'to be sure, to be sure'. You sure as hell can't be sure after only one 'to be sure'.

However, crack on we did, with the CEO opening the meeting. But I was struggling to pay attention as I'd been distracted by two of the men, each with take-out coffees and unopened bakery bags in front of them. What was in the bags?

As if to answer me, one man tore along the crease of the folded bag to reveal...

...an enormous scone. I swear it was almost the size of the Blarney Stone. And rather than being spotted with currants and raisins, it was patched in pink. He tipped out a small pat of wrapped butter and a plastic knife, set the scone onto the bag, and cut into it. The CEO seemed oblivious to this impromptu picnic.

Observing his colleague buttering his scone, the second man also tore open his bag, revealing the same - another monolith of a pink scone, butter and knife.

The CEO was about to hand over to me but before I could start, one of the scone-men piped up. 'Would anyone like some of me cherry scone? I've cut it into quarters and buttered it.'

I expected everyone to decline discreetly, as per the unwritten rules of a business meeting, but oh no, I'm somewhere where the ordinary rules don't apply.

Yes, they'd all like a bit of scone. Could someone pop out and get some napkins, someone asked, and a cup of tea would be nice, they said. And so, we spent the next 20 minutes with eight people munching on pink scones and talking about absent Niamh's baby.

In the end, the meeting was relatively successful, despite the high number of impromptu breaks for cigarettes, cups of tea and trips to the bakery.

When I got home, I checked in with my colleague who'd recommended me for the role, telling her about scone and maternity-gate.

'It's always like that there,' she said. 'You get used to it.'

So it would seem this is my new life, Bri.

Much love

Alison

**26 February 2012**

Alison visits with a box of scones, jam and cream – she says they're a secret Irish remedy. She said she's absolutely not going back into corporate world, but she said it so many times I think she may protest too much. She dodged questions about Dorset life, I noticed. However, she is going to join me in my new passion – alkalising. I've read that cancer thrives in an acidic body, so I'm on a mission to make mine all alkaline. Interestingly, lemons are alkaline, as is anything green, so I'm guzzling vile, green liquid like my life depends on it, which I guess it probably does. I pee every day onto pH sensitive paper and hope the result is alkaline. In a show of support, Neil is also peeing daily onto the paper but, irritatingly, despite not 1 drop of green juice passing his lips, he is naturally alkaline. Alison is joining the peeing massif and has taken home a box too.

### 11 March 2012 – North Hampshire Hospital, Basingstoke

Appointment with Miss W at Cutting Edge. The scan shows the liver has grown back to 90% its original size. 90% in 6 weeks! I think the vile green liquid has been important in this. She is happy. Neil is happy. I am happy. And she will discharge me. I'll be sad to leave her care and I thanked her for being so efficient and making it all so easy. I think she had a tear in her eye. Neil asked if it was OK for me to fly to South Africa. She said as long as it's business class. I like her immensely.

### 16 March 2012 – North Hampshire Hospital, Basingstoke

Back at Cutting Edge for discharge from consultant surgeon's clinic. He spoke very highly of Miss W – think we all have a crush on her.

Then it turned ugly. He said my oncologist may want me to undergo a series of chemo. No one has mentioned this before. I thought I was chemo resistant. I pretended I'd not heard and checked if I'm OK to fly. He said yes, so I am going on holiday. I am. I am. I am. I want to jump for joy about the holiday and wail about the chemo. I do neither but instead shake his hand and leave.

**17 March 2012**

Today I wailed.

Uncontrollable floods of snotty tears. I felt guilty. I should be happy. They've cut out the cancer; perhaps it won't even return. I can go on holiday. So why do I feel so sorry for myself? So bitterly, disappointingly, angrily, pathetically sorry for myself?

# CHAPTER EIGHTEEN

## HOPE OR HOPELESS?

**18 March 2012 – South Africa**

The fear that my scar may explode on the plane did not come true. I had imagined my side bloating with the pressure, just like feet do, and suddenly my newly grown liver splurting out all over the dinner tray. The reality is we have arrived in Cape Town without incident. And now I sit on the balcony, in shorts, sipping fresh orange juice, thinking how lucky I am to be here. Lucky? Really? Yes, lucky.

**19 March 2012 – South Africa**

Last night a huge man, with bloodshot eyes and gaping mouth, climbed through the bedroom window and tried to smother me with a pillow. I struggled to push him off but was fighting a losing battle. I cried out for help but no one came. I woke up in a pool of sweat, Neil holding me, saying everything was OK, telling me it was a dream. But it felt so real. It still does.

**20 March 2012 – South Africa**

Never had a penthouse suite before. The decking is like the bow of a ship, looking out over the ocean. I feel like Jack and Rose in Titanic. I resist the urge to recreate the scene with Neil! Or even tell him. He's still struggling to get his head round my burst-scar-in-plane worry. All I need to tell him is that I am happy. And I am.


## 22 March 2012 – South Africa

I so want to go swimming. In the mirror I look like Frankenstein's monster – a body made up of different parts that have been stitched together. The old scar is beginning to fade but the new one is glaring. I won't be going swimming. I told Neil I thought the scar would sting. He went in and I paddled on the edge.

Tonight he told me that my scars are now part of my history. They show what I have survived and I should be proud. Which of course is true. But... But what? I don't know. I am changed.


## 23 March 2012 – South Africa

Neil suggested canoeing today. I wouldn't have canoed even in the BC era. But he'd got it all sussed. A double canoe; he'd paddle. No deep water, he promised. He reminded me I am alive and I need to act like it. Feel like that girl Alison used to work with taking stones out of a pocket each time she went outside her comfort zone.

Water was calm, the views of the beaches wonderful and the sun nourishing. Then it all went wrong – we ran aground. I panicked, thinking I'd have to jump out, swim and my scar would split, and I'd watch my innards float away before me. Neil told me I needed to get out of the canoe. I couldn't. I froze. He cajoled and coaxed and eventually I swung out my shaking legs and dropped into the sea. Up to my knees!

On the way back we stopped at a cove. I wrote a message in the sand.

# HOPE & LOVE

As we paddled away, I sent a silent prayer to the universe and then turned to watch a wave wash away my words.

**21 March 2012**

Hi Brian

I know you're on holiday but I wanted a letter to be waiting for you on your return. I hope South Africa has washed away some of your frustrations, anxiety and upset, if that's possible.

Even though I say I want to write a letter, I don't actually have anything to report so instead I'll update you on how alkalizing is going:

First pH test 7.5. I'm delighted - nicely alkaline.

Next day pH 5.5. I'm horrified - I've gone acidic overnight.

Next day pH 8. I'm delighted - back on track.

Next day pH 6.5. I'm confused.

And this is all while I'm on my super-healthy, eat-lots-of-veggies regime. I'm thinking this peeing on pH paper may not be too reliable. Of course, all this isn't of prime importance to me but it is to you, Bri. So, I think you perhaps need to get your blood tested if you want an accurate reading, and not rely on these pesky piss sticks. However, every cloud has a silver lining – you may want to let Neil 'I'm so alkaline I don't even have to try' know that he may not be as alkaline as he thinks and so can stop alkaline-shaming the rest of us.

The other thing that is rather unreliable is my ability to maintain my alkaline diet while living a normal life. Other foods, which all taste and look more delicious, keep getting in the way

Tea Taster and I were taken out by our lovely friends, Vics and Robert, for a belated engagement dinner. They've been engaged for such a long time that no one, including them, can remember when or where Robert actually proposed, so there were no badgering questions about us setting a date for our wedding.

Vics and I made a sterling attempt to mimic the drinking feats of our singleton days, ordering and downing every alcoholic beverage the restaurant had to offer. The boys happily joined in the challenge and by the time the waiter came to take our order I couldn't even say alkaline, let alone select an appropriate pH dish. As it turned out, the restaurant had been on the go since the 70's and was still stuck there – the menu boasted chicken kiev, scampi and black forest gateau. Unfortunately, the prices were not stuck in the 70's but instead positively acidic, so our friends paid a fortune for our mushy veg, white rice and deep fried everything.

At the end of the meal, Vics slung her arm round me and said/slurred, 'You know, if I wasn't engaged, I'd make a pass at Robert. Isn't he gorgeous?'

I reminded her that she was engaged to Robert.

'Oh, yes.' She sighed. 'Shame.'

We were even more drunk than I thought.

I'm now back on the pH campaign again and will try not to fall from grace again.

Much love

Alison

**24 March 2012**

Hi Brian

As you read this, I hope to be lying on a sunbed in Egypt. We've got a rare child-free five days and are rushing off to the sun.

Previously, our holidays have only ever been long weekends due to childcare but the brevity of the trips has never stopped Tea Taster from getting into the vibe of the location. In our first round of dating, we went to New York. Tea Taster had never been before so was beside himself with glee, and I mean glee! Each morning we'd go to the diner near the hotel, each morning I'd order my sunny-side-up eggs and coffee and each morning he'd order his waffles, bacon and juice, and then after a pause would say, in his best New York accent, 'And I'll take a cworfeee please.'

Each morning the waitress would stare in confusion.

'Sorry, sir?'

'Oh, just a coffee please,' he'd mumble.

And as if this wasn't enough, on one occasion, as we passed a sports shop in which was a group of swaggering, black boys in hoodies, he called out, 'How ya doin?' trying to mirror their swagger.

The boys scowled, until they spotted his chinos and blazer, laughed and called back, 'Yo dude, how you doin'?' They all came over to high-five the Englishman, invited him to a baseball match and he, in return, offered his address should they ever be in Dorset and fancy popping in.

On a weekend in Marrakech, Tea Taster loved the souks but, with the orientation skills of a whirling top, could not venture in alone. He delighted in the market stalls, choosing a pair of slippers, bartering as if his life depended on it and then saying, 'No thank you, sir – not today.' I came to realise that he was addicted to souk shopping. Every day we went through the same routine: stop at stall, choose slippers, barter, say not today, thank you. On the final day, when he actually did want to buy slippers, I, fed up with his bizarre form of retail therapy, sent him out alone. Four hours later he crawled back to the hotel, weighed down with slippers, saying he'd bartered too hard!

So, you can imagine the joys that Egypt may hold for us!

However, before I sign off and start to pack my suitcase, I must tell you about my most interesting experience of the week.

Yesterday, I took Lizzie to the kennels for the days we'll be away. As I put on her lead, she jumped around, anticipating a walk. I told her we were going to the kennels but as I don't speak 'dog' she just wagged her tail and yelped in excitement. Of course, her joy heightened when she spotted the car; a car journey for Lizzie usually means a trip to the beach.

I shook my head.

'No walking today, Lizzie.'

She spun round on the seat in a delighted frenzy.

As I drove, I fretted. How could I make her understand she was going to the kennels, that the kennels had been chosen specially because they were part of a rescue centre, came highly recommended, and that in six days we'd come back to get her? I felt awful.

On arrival, Lizzie leapt out of the car, ready for her walk, but in reception she twigged all was not well and instead jumped onto my lap, snuggling into my sweater.

'It's OK, Lizzie,' I said, but it wasn't. The kennels were great, the girls kind, but I felt dreadful.

Of course, Brian, you must know how I felt because you love Colin. But I don't love Lizzie. I find her annoying; she begs for food at the table, I have to pick up her poo in the street and she attacks every dog she passes. Every time I leave Tea Taster's, my clothes are covered in dog hairs and if he comes to me for a weekend she has to come too.

I sometimes wish Lizzie belonged to another family. I hate that everything we do revolves around how long she can be left in the house on her own. But Family Hitchcock dote on the dog-attacking little mutt, so the chances of her ever being re-homed are zero.

And yet, there I was, feeling awful that going to the kennels was upsetting her and I couldn't let her know it would be OK.

Is this what happens in families, Brian? You feel a sense of responsibility? I know Brené Brown said we need to be vulnerable to connect but she never mentioned pets. Is this my future?

Lots of love, Brian. Thinking of you.

Much love

Alison

**24 March 2012**

Back home with a bump. Letters on the door mat. Two from Alison and one from the hospital. Appointment this week with the oncologist. Don't expect he'll remember me.

**26 March 2012**

Feel very alone today as Neil goes to work and the streets are quiet as everyone gets on with their lives. I wash holiday clothes but by this afternoon I'm despondent and fearing tomorrow's hospital appointment. I make a cup of tea and settle down with Alison's 2 letters. Before I know it, I'm in a souk in Marrakesh.

**30 March 2012 – King Edward VII Hospital, Windsor**

Oncologist didn't get up when we entered his office nor even look up. But he probably didn't want to look me in the eye. My T cells are too weak for more chemo, so that means nothing to kill off any rogue cells and he's pretty sure the cancer will emerge again. A 'strong possibility', he said. But we won't know till after the scan. In 4 months' time. What happened to hope?

**31 March 2012**

Couldn't sleep last night. Awful pain in my right side. Sweat drenching the bed clothes. Tried to work out which organ it must be. Which organ the cancer was creeping into. Then I farted and the pain disappeared.

**1 April 2012**

I am spending too much time on the internet.

I start off researching lifestyle options for people living with cancer and before I know it, I'm down a rabbit hole of stage IV cancer survivors' blogs, inspirational quotes and scented candles.

Apparently, I should be:

- Grateful for where I am right now rather than where I'd hoped to be.
- Grateful to be alive and have all I need for today.
- Grateful not to know the future.

They can all piss off.

I return to Facebook for pictures of kittens.

**2 April 2012**

Bit of good news – Penny Brohn has had a cancellation (I wonder if this comes due to a death?) and I can get on the second part of the Living Well Course. I have a list of questions. No more internet.

Think I will call in on Alison on the way there – see if she's brought me some sunshine from her holiday. I'm expecting she'll at least have come back with a date set for the wedding.

**3 April 2012**

Hi Brian

I'm back from sunny Egypt. But, of course, you know this as by the time you receive this letter, you'll have popped in on your way to Penny Brohn. I'll be up to date on your news but I shall have kept my news for this letter. I hope Penny Brohn can work its magic and help you to learn to live, in some way, with all the uncertainty you face now. Never apologise for sending a ranting or frustrated text or email. It's what friends are for.

So, how was Egypt, I hear you ask? I was so looking forward to doing nothing other than lying on a sunbed, reading a book and sipping cocktails. Tea Taster's idea of a perfect holiday is somewhat different. He'd packed his Dummies Guide to hieroglyphics and archaeologist's notebook!

Unsurprisingly, the Arab Spring had frightened off most tourists. This meant the souvenir vendors were struggling more than ever. This, of course, put Tea Taster in the firing line for every shop-keeper, hawker and taxi driver. Also, having an attitude was not his forte. As we know, Tea Taster is one of life's gentle-folk, and the hawkers could smell this a mile off.

On the first night, my dear fiancé insisted we have a romantic stroll by the Nile. I would rather have stayed in the hotel bar but I needed to be better at being part of a holidaying-couple so agreed. As a blonde, and having visited before, I was well accustomed to seeing off all sellers and horse and carriage taxi drivers. But it seemed my display of easy authority lulled Tea Taster into a false sense of security as the next morning he announced he was off to a temple. I announced I was off to a sun-lounger. He looked disappointed but not discouraged.

Hours later, a broken man returned to the hotel.

'I have never experienced anything like it,' he said, slumping onto the neighbouring sun-lounger and gulping down my mid-afternoon gin and tonic. 'They wouldn't leave me alone. Look!'

He held up a bag full of postcards, mini sphinxes and pharaoh heads. Things had got so bad that an Egyptian woman had given him advice.

'Tell them no. You are too nice. Too nice Englishman.'

She quickly followed this up with a request for £5.

It seemed Tea Taster's only friend was Ahmed, a horse and carriage driver. He'd given a 'good price' for safe passage back to the hotel but only on the understanding that he'd be used for all future trips out.

Tea Taster's daily sightseeing trips continued, as did my days lounging by the pool. I'm not sure that's how you're supposed to spend holidays with your fiancé but it's what we did.

On the penultimate evening, I relented and agreed go out for dinner. Our hotel stood back from the road, a sweeping, red-carpeted staircase leading down to the mass of taxis and sellers below. As we stepped out, a sea of faces looked up, spotted who had emerged and together cried out, 'Mr Hitch, Mr Cock.'

Tea Taster waved back, like a Hollywood superstar.

'They all know you?' I cried.

'Oh, yes,' replied the A-Lister.

At the bottom of the steps, we were pounced upon, each driver claiming he had been promised a fare, but Ahmed had first dibs and so, ignoring the pleas of other drivers, we climbed into his carriage. Half way there, the driver turned to ask something and Tea Taster realised he was not Ahmed. It was too late to do anything, we having negotiated a 'there and back' rate, so we sat tight and hoped the real Ahmed would never find out. But that was never going to happen. Once back, we faced his full wrath.

'Mr Hitch, Mr Hitch. You promise. What happen? We make deal.'

A shamed Mr Hitch paled, mumbled an apology and scurried into the safety of the hotel.

'We forgot to buy a bottle of water,' I said when we reached the room.

'Oh no!' Tea Taster dropped his head into his hands. 'I can't go out there again. I'll be lynched. Don't make me go out there. You'll just have to go thirsty.'

On our last night, in the safety of the hotel restaurant, we talked weddings. It seems Tea Taster wants a wedding this year. And I want one vaguely sometime in the future. We've not mentioned it since. A holiday of compromise is one thing, but a marriage quite another.

In the middle of all our 'holiday fun', I forgot the anniversary of my dad's death. I felt guilty but I guess what really matters is he's not generally forgotten.

I'm reading a book that is the diary of a woman born in 1901. She wrote from the age of 13 to when she died in the early 1990s. Of course, her story is remarkable in that it spans a century, but each entry is ordinary and every day. And it is only her story. Everyone's story is just their own and whatever you do in life your story goes with you when you are no more. This made me think how important it is to make the most of our stories while we're here. Do you remember this Mark Twight quote:

'Eventually, I sickened of people, myself included, who didn't think enough of themselves to make something of themselves – people who did only what they had to do and never what they could have done. I learned from them the infected loneliness that comes at the end of every misspent day. I knew I could do better.'

Thinking about it now, I realise how grateful we should be to be part of other people's stories. Without your story, I would never have discovered my love of writing and without Tea Taster's story, this letter would have no content. I wonder what stories Penny Brohn will give you.

Off now, Brian. I have much Egyptian tat to arrange on my mantelpiece.

Much love

Alison

**3 April 2012 – Penny Brohn Cancer Care, Bristol**

Sabrine is my new best friend. I met her at breakfast this morning. We're pretty much in the same place with our cancers – the bowel/liver tribe. She raves about the wonders of juicing, guzzles matcha green tea as if she were Japanese and mediates as she walks. She is in her 30s, petite and has a look of Audrey Hepburn. I am mesmerized by her and feel calm in her presence. I vow to do more of what she does to help myself.

This evening we had an art class. Shame it's too late for Alison's art auction. I was hoping for a bit of life drawing, perhaps with a nude male model – a treat for us all. Instead, we were asked to breathe and visualise and 'share with the paper'. One woman explained painting made her feel alive and positive. She asked what my painting was about. I couldn't bring myself to say the black and yellow splodges were my cancer so I said it was a sunrise. She said that was very uplifting. It wasn't. Sabrine overheard and winked at me. She'd painted a young boy.

**4 April 2012 – Penny Brohn Cancer Care, Bristol**

I am full of information after meeting with the doctor here. She recommended the book Forks over Knives, which will set me off on the right nutritional path, and suggested walking should be my only exercise. Anything more strenuous will put my body under stress, weaken the immune system and prevent the T cells from killing the cancer cells – they will be too busy fighting off inflammation and infections. Wow – who knew? So it's goodbye charming Steve and hello Colin.

### 5 April 2012 – Penny Brohn Cancer Care, Bristol

I am sad to be leaving today. Life is so much easier here. Healthy food, which is planned and cooked for you, like-minded people, never needing to explain why you feel what you feel, but most of all, oodles of positive energy. But I head off with a renewed motivation to look at what I eat, how I exercise and what my mind and body needs. And I have a new guiding light in Sabrine.

### 8 April 2012

Easter is not easy on my new diet of green leafy vegetables, juice and no sugar.

Sugar-free hot-cross buns are acceptable but not delicious and the no chocolate thing is killing me (or hopefully not).

A green powder called Super Greens is my Easter egg of choice. I mix it with water until it resembles something I've scooped out of the pond and then I hold my nose and gag/glug it/throw it down my throat. On the upside, it promises to alkalise me and I've not had to chop any vegetables. Both Alison and Neil have declined to drink it as part of their 'support Brian' alkalising regime.

**12 April 2012**

I am the proud owner of a state-of-the-art juicer, as recommended by Sabrine, and my bank account is £300 lighter. I'll need to make a lot of juice to make this purchase worthwhile. Just need to work out how to fit it all together first. You'd think for £300 it would arrive with a nice man who constructs it for you and makes your first glass.

Today's juice:

- 1 apple
- 1 pear
- 1/2 a cucumber
- 1/2 a bag of kale
- 1 small piece of ginger

It's very very green. (It looks green, is green and tastes green)

**14 April 2012 – London**

Delighted to be fitting back into my black tie of 15 years ago for Gillian's swanky birthday bash. Another positive of this new anti-cancer regime. And a positive that I'm there for Gillian, doing something for her, rather than the other way round. But my bubble of joie de vivre burst when a doctor at the party said I could be doing more harm than good as none of this nutritional 'nonsense' has been tested nor scientifically proven. Surely it's better than doing nothing, isn't it?

**18 April 2012**

Can't do with anymore daytime TV. It's all so squeaky clean, positive and bonkers. Today, a woman cheated on her alien partner with another alien and a man can't work out how to rehome his homing pigeons. What the hell. Never appreciated that a job provides so much social connection and saves you from the horror of this rubbish.

Ruth has suggested I volunteer at the Cancer Research UK shop. Distract me, fill my day, get me out of the house. Stress-free. It's a long way from tax accountant to high-flying ex-pats. I haven't worked in a shop since I had a Saturday job in John Coliers Gentleman's Outfitters in Cardiff – purveyors of the casual slack.

**23 April 2012 – Cancer Research Charity Shop, Sunningdale**

My first day back in retail after 39 years. A morning's trial shift. I was nervous.

I'm put on processing with Sheila (75). Pat (78) is keeper of the till, perched behind the counter on a bar stool. Doreen (78) is security. Last week they had a Thelma and Louise style shoe heist – a pair of hardly worn Laboutin's and a get-away car. We're all overseen by manager Julie (no age disclosed).

The morning went quickly, the ladies were friendly and I passed my trial shift – I am now officially a volunteer. And part of the geriatric brigade.

**24 April 2012 – Village Hall, Sunningdale**

Ruth has also suggested Tai Chi in the church hall with 10 elderly ladies. Why did I think this was a good idea? I'd enjoyed Tai Chi at Penny Brohn but I felt a bit of a misfit with this lot – there's only so many older ladies you want in your life per week. I persevered and did begin to relax but it's not for me. The energy is all wrong. Did I really write that? Back to daytime TV. How have I gone from boozy city lunches with like-minded, ambitious work colleagues to the life of a geriatric?

**8 May 2012**

I am missing wonderful Penny Brohn, especially Sabrine: the inspiration, positivity and lightness of spirit. Here at home, I lurch from one day to the next, wading through the fug. A good day is one when I don't cry.

**9 May 2012**

Wrote a new will this morning.

Out goes UNICEF and RNLI, and in comes Cancer Research UK and Penny Brohn.

**11 May 2012**

It must be shit being Neil with me around. I may not be dead but his life is so diminished. Cancelled supper with the neighbours. Can't face everyone being jolly. Neil went alone. Better off without me. Instead,

I sat down and wrote a letter to Sabrine. I told her about the geriatric brigade, the difference a sweet apple can make to a juice and my days of fug. It was like she was there with me, in the room, chatting, listening, understanding. Maybe Brené Brown has a point.

Didn't even hear Neil coming to bed.

# CHAPTER NINETEEN

## HOWLING AT THE MOON

2004 Conference
of Traffic Psychology & Technology

**20 May 2012**

Dear Brian

Very pleased to hear you have a new alkalizing friend (Sabrine, not the juicer). Does that mean I can stand down? I don't know how you keep it going, Brian. I know it's healthy but all those vegetables! I miss cake. And wine. And nice things. You and Sabrine go for your lives (don't read that the wrong way).

I was meant to meet Natasha this week to talk all things wedding but had to cancel. She says I'm procrastinating but I'm really not. We haven't even set a date so there really is no rush. I have new tenants moving into my East London flat and needed to remove the packaging of the recently delivered furniture.

'Don't worry. I'll get rid of the packaging,' I said to my kind neighbour who had taken delivery, imagining it to be just a bin-liner of a few bits of cardboard.

The next day, I trotted off to the flat and up the narrow spiral staircase to pick up the expected bag from my 4th floor flat.

Now, if for one nano-second I had given any thought to the packaging that may be left from the delivery of a three-seater sofa and a double bed, I would have realised that I was about to be faced with something more than a bin-liner full of cardboard.

As I stepped into the flat, I saw what I was truly faced with. There in front of me was indeed a bin-liner full of cardboard – an-eight-feet high and three-feet-wide one. How on earth was I going to get this down the stairs, and then, when I did get it down the stairs, where was I going to put it? It's not like I could take it on the Tube with me to deposit in some suitable dump in Chiswick – I had no clue where you dump your over-sized cardboard packaging in Bethnal Green.

While contemplating this oversized body-bag of cardboard, I noticed that the smoke alarm was bleeping. On the outside was a sticker saying that the battery could not be replaced.

I couldn't get it to stop bleeping and my tenant was due to move in within the next half hour. In a bit of a panic, I unscrewed it, still bleeping, and stuffed it into my handbag. I then started to drag the cardboard-filled body-bag down the stairs. Oh my God, Bri, if you could have seen me. It took me at least 20 minutes to get it down the four flights. When I finally did get down to the street, I dragged the bag behind me, all eight feet of it, and finally dumped it outside Iceland. And then scurried away.

Of course, my embarrassment didn't end there. Because remember, Bri, I was about to get on the Tube with a bleeping smoke alarm in my handbag. I must have changed trains five times more than I needed to, just so that no one got so suspicious that they pulled the emergency cord and had me arrested!

It's debatable as to whether I was any more suspicious than the woman carrying a bag with '2004 - Conference of Traffic Psychology and Technology' printed on it. Or the bloke choosing to sit on his own camp chair rather than the normal seats. We were an eclectic mix on the Tube that day!

I'd been so looking forward to being back in London but not to the challenges of an eight-foot body bag of cardboard. I'd be better off in Dorset - and that's saying something!

Much love

Alison

**24 May 2012**

Natasha is right, Alison is wedding dodging. Feel I should help but I have more set on helping myself right now. What kind of friend does that make me? All I'm good for is hanging out with the oldies in the charity shop.

**25 May 2012**

Once you've had a cancer diagnosis it stays with you for good. It may not be at the front of your mind all the time but it's definitely always lurking. Life will never return to what it was. The only people who seem to understand this are other people with cancer.

**3 June 2012**

Hi Brian

I can't guarantee the quality of this letter as I'm writing at Tea Taster's house. Billy's screaming at his Xbox, Alfie's banging out some hip tunes on his phone and Tea Taster's extolling the virtues of his latest bottle of sherry. I very much doubt the muse can be with me. I'm also questioning why I turned down Natasha's invitation to a glamourous celebrity-laden party in London in favour of a weekend in Dorset. There was even a rumour that Prince Harry may have made an appearance. But too late now – I've made my choice!

On Saturday afternoon, after Tea Taster had gone cycling, two policemen turned up on the doorstep. My heart stopped for a moment, until they asked if I was Alfie's mother and was he in. Of course, I had no idea where Alfie was but Billy informed them that he'd probably be hanging around the skate park. The policemen said they had reason to believe he had actually been hanging around the disused public toilets.

'Graffiti?' Billy asked as he did a spin-kick in the doorway and bowed to the police. What?

'He's right. We believe Alfie Hitchcock has been spray painting the public toilets with male genitalia and associated slogans.'

Associated slogans!

I was about to protest, in a panic, that they needed proof but then heard the words 'CCTV' and 'words spelt incorrectly'. Oh God, Alfie's dyslexia was known to the local police and had outed him as the culprit.

'It's happened before,' snitched Billy, unhelpfully. 'Will he go to prison this time?'

The police said probably not but they'd like to speak to him at the station and would I mind accompanying them into town to find him and be his 'appropriate adult'?

No. No. No, my mind screamed. I don't even know what an appropriate adult is, let alone how to be one.

'Alison will be our step-mum soon,' Billy said, again unhelpfully. And so, the rest of my Saturday was spent in the police station listening to Alfie being given a caution and dressing down, which was clearly as much aimed at me, his step-mother-to-be, as it was at him.

By the time Tea Taster returned from his bike ride, we were home, Alfie sulking in his bedroom at the grounding he knew was to come. Billy did a Taekwondo routine to celebrate his brother being in trouble but little did he know his own horror was yet to come.

Billy has a new girlfriend but it's all a bit hush hush as her dad doesn't allow her to have boyfriends. She and Billy had swapped mobile numbers and Billy had texted her to say 'hi'. Moments later, his phone rang, number withheld. Billy answered and a girl, with a Welsh accent, asked who she was speaking to. Billy thought his new girlfriend was playing games so he replied, in a Welsh accent, that it was Billy and he was missing her. The phone went dead.

A few minutes later it rang again, this time with a man's voice shouting down the phone, 'Who is this?'

Billy, frightened, ended the call.

'Do you think that was Emily's Dad?' he asked. 'He sounded really angry.'

Family Hitchcock then went into overdrive – how dare the father phone Billy, scaring him? Alfie, apparently, knew people who could sort him out. Tea Taster's mum, a counsellor, thought the family may have issues. Tea Taster advised Billy to turn off the phone and go to bed. But before he could, a text came through: 'If I find out who you are I'm going to kick the shit out of you.'

Billy threw the phone into the air and ran out of the room.

'What a terrible family she's got. I'd dump her,' advised Tea Taster.

'He's got anger issues,' said his mum.

'Leave it with me, I'll sort it,' said Alfie, forgetting he was grounded.

'Pass me the paper that Emily wrote her number on please,' I said to Billy.

Sure enough, Billy had copied the number into his phone with one digit incorrect. He hadn't been texting Emily at all. He'd been breaking up a marriage in Wales.

Fortunately, Billy had gone to bed by the time the next text came through. 'I know who you are and where you live, you little prick.'

Another couple become a statistic in the government's failing drive to keep families together.

The next morning, Billy said he couldn't go to school as he had stomach ache. Tea Taster had already departed for work so I was left to sort it out. I asked him if he'd like some toast with extra jam. After three slices and his stomach ache clearly forgotten, I coaxed out the real

problem. He said he was too embarrassed to see
Emily after the phone debacle. I pointed out
that Emily didn't actually know anything about
it so it could stay our secret. Billy then said
he should probably go to school, in case Emily
was missing him.

Tea Taster says he can't wait for me to move in
once we're married!

Much love, Brian

Alison

**8 June 2012 – London**

Date with Sabrine. She brought me Kris Carr's Crazy Sexy Diet cancer
book. She said it was a thank you for the letter, which she didn't need
to do. She said it was the nicest thing anyone had done for her in ages.
It never really occurred to me that the mesmerizing Sabrine feels as
alone as I do.

We talked and talked. I don't have anyone else who so completely
gets me. I feel seen.

We're pretty much in the same place as regards to our conventional
treatments but she's way ahead of me on the alternative front; I need
to up my game. Just as well I'm off to Bristol for complementary

therapy advice from Dr H tomorrow. Think I may have become cancer competitive?

### 9 June 2012

I am officially a Kris Carr devotee. She's lived with stage IV cancer for almost 10 years. Her blog is full of easy ways to be healthier, smarter and positive. Thank you, Sabrine, for introducing me to Kris.

### 12 June 2012 – Bristol

So nice to see Dr H again. I feel in very safe hands. She thinks now's the time for the Hungarian dog medicine. I think what she really means is that we're at the stage where there's little to lose. It is actually a natural combination of Sodium Salicylate, Copper Gluconate, Manganese Gluconate and Ascorbic Acid (Vitamin C) taken in tablet form. It is unlicensed in the UK but she has several patients using it and has seen some great results. I left with the private prescription and ordered it straight away before I could change my mind. I wonder if Sabrine knows about it? I'll drop her a line to ask. Alison will be very amused and expect me to start howling at the moon no doubt.

### 17th June 2012

Another birthday, another year survived. And 4 months without surgery or treatment. 4 months of just trying to navigate this new life. Sometimes this seems harder than the treatment.

Neil's gift: a flight for us both to visit Chris and Philip in France.

### 23 June 2012 – France

It's not easy being a Hungarian dog medicine drug addict on holiday in someone else's home. Keep sloping off to the bedroom. I don't want anyone to see how many pills I'm taking, and not a single one licensed! Philip's already told me he thinks I could be doing more harm than good with my eating regime.

### 24 June 2012 – France

Out for dinner at one of our favourite restaurants. Well, it used to be a favourite. Barely anything on the menu I could eat. I told the waiter I am a vegetarian. He shrugged. It was suggested at the table that I drop the diet while I'm on holiday.

I ordered salad for starter and veggies and fries for my main but, as we split the bill equally, I still paid for champagne, wine, foie gras, duck, steak, lamb and desserts!

### 25 June 2012 – France

I don't want to be on holiday. Cancer may not be in my body but it's still in my head. I lost it when Neil told me not to spoil things by being morose. I ran out of the house and down the lane. At the end, when I realised there was nowhere to go, I slunk back. I apologised, and dived into the pool. Lap after lap after lap.

### 27 June 2012 – North Hampshire Hospital, Basingstoke

Blood Test Day. They're good here at the harpooning. Cutting Edge is a place filled with memories – all the scans, surgeries, consultations and tears. So many tears. I was in and out as quickly as I could, just leaving behind that small vial of blood. Next week is the CT scan and then scanxiety.

### 29 June 2012 – North Hampshire Hospital, Basingstoke

Scan day. If I don't write about it then perhaps it will be like it didn't happen. Even though it fills my mind – an inflating balloon, pushing all other thoughts out.

### 1 July 2012

Waiting. Waiting. Waiting.

Bloody scan results.

Feel sick. All the time.

Like I'm waiting for a balloon to burst.

### 2 July – 2012

Nora Ephron died last week.

She once said, 'The honest truth is that it's sad to be over 60.'

I wonder if I'll ever know.

Nora was the queen of the pithy statement.

'Death doesn't really feel eventual or inevitable. It still feels avoidable somehow. But it's not. We know in one part of our brains that we are all going to die, but on some level, we don't quite believe it.'

I do.

**7 July 2012**

Dear Brian

I know my letters are now less frequent and I'm disappointed with myself for that. If I'm not sorting out family problems in Dorset then I'm busy in Ireland herding cats – sorry, I mean working.

I've been given a team of two: Connor, who is an absolute star and works like a demon. And Siobhan, who arrives late for everything and eats big, fat buttered scones throughout meetings, leaving a trail of squashed currants in her wake.

Siobhan is the most hopeless person I've ever worked with. She was due to interview someone for a vacancy yesterday but she cancelled them. When I asked why she said:

'I'd noticed they had beavers listed as a hobby. When I asked them about it, they said they had 40. And so can't do interviews on Tuesday evenings. Due to the beavers.'

'Right,' I said, watching her stuff yet another scone into her mouth. 'And this makes them unsuitable for our job because...?'

'Well, I told them I thought they might be happier in a zoo or something. They didn't sound very keen but they clearly like animals. I mean, 40 beavers!'

I didn't bother to ask Siobhan if she'd ever heard of Scouts, Brownies, Cubs, Guides or Beavers.

And it seems craziness isn't limited to the staff. Last week, a client called to say they were very impressed with both the applicants they'd interviewed and as they were unable to choose between them, they'd decided to look at their hobbies to help with the decision-making.

'Once we saw the hobbies, the choice was obvious,' they said. 'We've chosen the applicant who listed washing elephants.'

This rather unusual animal theme continued in my taxi to the airport, on the radio. The feature was listeners' letters being read out on air.

'I agree with your listener last week who found it distasteful to watch a homosexual couple canoodling on a train,' read out the presenter. 'I too watched a couple doing the same yesterday, except that one of them was a woman, and I didn't enjoy it. However, I also have to admit that I lead a rather joyless life, so this could account for my reaction.'

The next letter read: 'Being homosexual will be outlawed once it goes out of fashion, which will probably be soon.'

The presenter ended the feature with the comment that the last letter was ridiculous, and that homosexuality would never go out of fashion as animals were also homosexual, and so proving it isn't a fad.

I received your lovely postcard today from France but was sad to hear you're struggling to deal with the 'living with cancer' limbo-land. I remembered our recent conversation over lunch: your new healthy regimes and alternative therapies. But all the regimes in the world can't remove niggling voices of uncertainty.

Over a glass of wine last week, I met up with the ex-colleague who had recommended me for the Ireland contract (I wasn't sure whether I should be buying the drinks to thank her or she should be buying them to apologise).

However, we'd really met up to toast my engagement. She wanted to hear about wedding plans and family life in Dorset. I told her I didn't really want to talk about it.

While other people see this as a cue to don a concerned face and dig to find the root of my silence, she merely nodded and said, 'That's OK.' I didn't have to explain, justify nor seek understanding. And so, I'd like to pass on that gift to you, Brian.

Your concerns will come and they will go, but let no one judge you for it or demand to know why – and most of all, don't judge yourself.

Much love

Alison

**9 July 2012**

'Brian, could you come to the clinic on 17th July?' It was Linda on the phone. '10am be OK?'

She couldn't give me any more information. It's not her job to share bad news.

Death certainly feels inevitable now, Nora.

I rang Neil and asked him to come home. We clung to each other, crying. How the hell are we back here so soon? I haven't even had my 6 months' clear. My endeavours to help my body have failed. What a complete waste of time and money.

## 11 July 2012

My new game is: Guess Where the Cancer Is?'

Everyday a new twinge, a new location. I knew on holiday something was wrong but everyone told me to not worry. But I just knew it would come back. Bloody cancer. The oncologist was right after all. Bully for him. Spent this morning curled up in a ball on the bed. Am going back there now.

## 12 July 2012

I don't want to tell anyone how worried I am about the 17th. I don't want to tell anyone I even have an appointment. I don't want to say any of it out loud. Alison's last letter said: 'let no one judge you for it or demand to know why – and most of all, don't judge yourself.'

She's right: this is not my fault. And I'll deal with it however I so choose.

**13 July 2012**

One sleepless night too many and I've snapped. I waited for Neil to leave the house and got on the phone. My stomach somersaulted; breakfast regurgitated into my throat.

Me: I know that you shouldn't tell me anything until I come into clinic on Friday and I understand completely if you decide not to say anything but I'm going crazy.

Colorectal Nurse Susie: You're right. I shouldn't and wouldn't ordinarily speak to you until after your appointment but as it's you, Brian, I will.

Shit – I hadn't been expecting that.

Me: Thank you.

Colorectal Nurse Susie: The scan shows a small shadow on your right lung – a small area of concern. It looks like everything else is clear. Just this one area. You can see the scan on Friday and we can refer you to a lung specialist. It's not lung cancer; it's a metastasis from the bowel cancer.

Be careful what you wish for. Now you know!

# CHAPTER TWENTY

## WHAT ABOUT THE BLOODY SMOKERS?

**17 July 2012**

What the fuck am I doing with cancer in my lung? What about all those bloody smokers? I am so fucking angry. The fucking injustice of it all. Yes, I know it's not technically lung cancer but what's the fucking difference? It's cancer in my lung. Don't fucking split hairs with me. As if the bowel and liver weren't enough. No, let's do everything in fucking threes. The world likes the order of things in threes. Well, I don't.

THIS CANCER CAN JUST FUCK OFF. IT'S TAKING THE PISS NOW.

And people can stop praising me for my passive acceptance of my plight.

FUCK OFF – I have had ENOUGH!

**17 July 2012**

Hi Brian

You're quiet so I thought I'd send you something to bring a bit of cheer. And, quite frankly, what is the point of me traipsing over to Ireland and doing all this work if I can't get some comedy stories out of it? To be sure, to be sure!

Last week, I spent the day in a meeting with a man who started every sentence with, 'I'm just asking the question, I'm not stating fact...' and would then state a fact with no question in sight.

Scones continue to haunt my life here. Stupidly, I'd thought their appearance in my meeting a few months ago was a one off, but no, it seems that whenever you eat or drink anything in Dublin, you accompany it with a scone. When I went to get lunch from the local take-out the other day, I was asked whether I wanted a plain or cheese scone with my soup. I said neither thank you, but this wasn't the right answer and so a scone was quickly stashed into my bag and I was sent on my way.

However, it seems that the general craziness may now be rubbing off on me.

Yesterday, I was due to have a breakfast meeting with the Board chair, Michelle – a woman who doesn't suffer fools, I was told. I woke up before my alarm, a chink of light creeping through the gap in the curtains. I love it when the light wakes you before your alarm gets a chance to. But the reason I love it is that it barely ever happens...

Oh shit. My alarm hadn't gone off. There was no way I was going to make the meeting, which had been due to start 15 minutes before I'd even woken up.

'Michelle, I'm so sorry,' I croaked down the phone. 'I can't get to the office to meet you, I'm afraid. I err, err, I can't leave the toilet. Terrible diarrhoea. Awful. So sorry.'

Diarrhoea? I'd said I'd got diarrhoea? What was wrong with migraine or food poisoning or even my alarm didn't go off?

Twenty minutes later, a knock on the door. The hotel porter handed over a brown paper bag.

'A gift. From Michelle,' he said.

Inside – four packs of Imodium.

Hopefully I won't need to go back for a couple
of weeks, if indeed they'll have me. Although
with their scones and my diarrhoea stories, I
actually think we're a good match!

Much love

Alison x

### 18 July 2012 – Southwold

Not sure I could do a whole three days being nice to people even if
they are Neil's family, but this was in the diary before cancer crept
into my lung so I'm not letting it spoil plans. I say we're not to tell
anyone what's happening to give us half a chance to enjoy being here.
And this is Neil's time – so few occasions now are about Neil. And
Colin will love the beach and sea, and be our faithful distraction. It
will be fine. I will make it fine.

### 19 July 2012 – Southwold

Picnic on the beach. 13 of us ranging from 8 to 76 years old. A real
family occasion. Neil laughed with his cousins – made me so happy to
see and then sad that I may not get to see it again.

When I felt it was too much, I took myself off for a walk with Colin.
That dog knows every emotion I have. We watched the family from
the other end of the beach. They shouted for me to come back to play

cricket. Colin and I ran. My shadowed lungs breathed. I ran. And ran. And ran again. Until I was breathless and sweaty. But alive.

**20 July 2012**

Left Southwold with positive energy. Opened the door back at home to discover Mr Angry in residence.

Don't want to leave the house or answer the phone. I can't trust what Mr Angry will say.

Other things Mr Angry won't do:

- Juice anything – just means he has to clean the bloody juicer.
- Drink any green gloop – tastes like shit.
- Meditate – can't sit still for long enough.
- Do yoga – all that talk of breathing makes him think about failing lungs.
- Pop vitamin pills – what's the point?

**21 July 2012**

Took Colin out for a walk, miles from home and familiar faces.

My Abel & Cole veg box turned up today. Left it on the doorstep.

**22 July 2012 – North Hampshire Hospital, Basingstoke**

Is a 7mm lesion the same as a 7mm tumour?

Will there be more lesions?
What is a lesion?
Am I going to die?
Why is this so much worse than the previous 2 times?
And what about the fucking smokers?

How could I have left my appointment and not know the answers to any of these questions?

Neil wants to tell people. People will think I'm dying and they won't know what to say. If he wants to tell people he can but I'm not.


**23 July 2012**

Stayed in the house all day. If I go out, there will be an outbreak of pitying, tilted heads.


**24 July 2012**

I planned to phone Alison to tell her the latest but I'm too ashamed. Ashamed of my body, ashamed of being the person with only bad news, ashamed that I don't want to hear her stories. Ashamed of the person I've become.


**25 July 2012**

Gillian and Alison both text today. Seems I've been so quiet they're worried I might be dead. I tell them about the lungs but say I don't want pity. Alison suggests I get myself involved in Olympic viewing. A distraction.

## 26 July 2012 – John Radcliffe Hospital, Oxford

I have put myself one notch above the tobacco-smoking lung cancer patients. Today's tests say my lungs are over 100% capacity for my age. No idea how I have lungs outperforming themselves but I'll take it as a positive. Must be all that walking with Colin.

## 27 July 2012

Have taken Alison's advice and am going large on the Olympic distraction.

Watched the opening ceremony with Luke and Charlotte, who are too young to remember the last Olympics so it was especially exciting for them. They settled on the sofa with fizzy drinks and popcorn and asked for the curtains to be closed to make it like the cinema. I had to keep leaving the room. Just couldn't stop my eyes filling up. But their joy was infectious and I smiled more than I cried. Alison was right about seeing the world through the eyes of a child.

## 28 July 2012 – Eton Dorney Lake: Olympic Rowing

I actually made it. When the tickets arrived a year ago I really wasn't sure I'd still be alive. It was all heats today so we saw plenty of action but it didn't really seem important who was rowing or who won. All that mattered was I was there.

**30 July 2012 – Guildford Hospital**

Today I starred in a 1950s sci-fi 'B' movie – Man and the Specialist Nuclear Medicine Unit. It's not a film I'll be recommending or watching again.

The nurse led me into a small cell-like room of grey walls with a concrete bench. No distracting pictures, soft furnishings or even a light. She wore something akin to a hazmat suit. In her hands: a tray with cannula, needles and vial of clear liquid.

The liquid was the radioactive dye that would attach itself to any lesions and glow in the scanner, so she told me. Stay away from pregnant women, small children and pets. So matter-of-fact. How many times a day does she say the same lines? No cuddles with Colin for a while.

I was injected and told to lie on the bench while the radioactive liquid streamed through my body. No music, magazines or books – just me, my thoughts and the dark. Too dark to even read one of Alison's letters. I realise now what good company they were through all those chemo sessions.

I imagined the toxic fluid flowing through my veins but that didn't feel like the sort of thing I should be visualizing. Reiki Ron would have had me on a beach, no doubt, so I imagined sand, crashing waves and a soothing breeze. And then I fell asleep. I think.

The scanner was 50 minutes of lying still with my arms above my head. I ached. I tried to get back to the beach but I couldn't find it. Too attached to my reality.

So now I wait for the results. How come we never get used to waiting?

**1 August 2012**

Today's distraction – the sewing machine. I'd forgotten how satisfying it is. A pair of purple velvet cushions for Gillian's new sofa. Professional job, though I do say so myself.

**3 August 2012**

Gillian loves the cushions. They will remind her of me when I'm no longer here.

Neither of us actually say this.

**4th August 2012**

Super Saturday at the Olympics is the best distraction. Medal after medal. Six golds. So much positive energy. Wonderful to watch years of training, sacrifice and desire resulting in something we can all be proud of. Of course, I spent most of the evening in tears – every win, every medal ceremony, every interview. Even the national anthem had me in floods.

Celebrating the medals meant we didn't need to celebrate our 5-year civil partnership anniversary. Couldn't cope with any more tears.

**5 August 2012**

Hi Brian

Wanted to get a letter to you before I go off on holiday, and while you're in need of distraction. I saw one of your 'fucking smokers' in the street the other day and I had to all but stop myself from running over and snatching the cigarette from his mouth.

I can't say I'm relishing the thought of our holiday in Cornwall with mine and Tea Taster's families. At least this time we're in accommodation that boasts more than one bedroom and no electricity meter. We will, however, have the joy of Billy inviting each of us to spin kick with him, being woken by my niece and nephew at 6am and being the first family down on the beach at 8.30am, all wrapped up in woolly jumpers and socks. My mum will be insisting she walks arm in arm with Tea Taster at all times.

Did I tell you what she said last time we were out?

For years now, since contracting her wibbly wobbly disease, my mum has walked very slowly, stick in one hand and holding onto mine or my sister's arm with the other. Out walking recently, my mum took Tea Taster's arm – I was somewhere behind carrying the bags. Tea Taster commented to my mum that when she gets going, she can walk at a good pace.

'Yes,' I heard her reply. 'Alison walks so slowly with me. I much prefer walking quicker.'

Fucking cheek.

On a jollier note, my mum, like us, Brian, has been completely swept up by the Olympics and surprised herself with her enthusiasm for it all. One person whose enthusiasm has surprised no one, is Tea Taster's. Oh, my Lord, never have I seen a man so excited.

He was lucky enough to go to the stadium on the first Friday night. I was unlucky enough to be watching TV with him the following night.

'We were sitting there,' he shouted, jumping up and pointing at the screen. 'Just to the right of that man's head.'

'So, we can't actually see where you were sitting?' I said.

'Well, yes, we were there – just off the screen.'

A few minutes later, there was a shot of the torch.

'Oh, oh,' squealed Tea Taster. 'We were just to the left of the torch. Just there, right there.'

'We can't actually see to the left of the torch,' I pointed out.

'Well, no, but we were there, just to the left of it. Oh, I wish I was back there. Amazing atmosphere. Amazing.'

And so our evening, and indeed the rest of our Olympic viewing, progressed. Every shot of the stadium is accompanied by a commentary of where Tea Taster had been sitting, what he could see and how he'd felt (always amazing).

Long camera shots of the Olympic Park prompted him to tell us where he'd walked, where he'd tried to buy a T-shirt, where he'd had his photo taken with Dame Tanni Grey-Thompson and where someone had dropped a disused ticket, which he'd picked up as a souvenir.

At no time can I be in Tea Taster's company and not be within ear or eye shot of the Olympics – laptop in the kitchen, stereo in the bedroom, TV in the living room, radio in the car, live commentary streaming through his phone. Every night, we check out the medal table before turning off the light.

Each time Team GB win a medal, he says how pleased he is, especially if it was one of his sports – Wiggins in the road cycling, Hoy in the track cycling, Farrah in the 10,000m and the Brownlee Brothers in the triathlon. Everyone who runs a 'good race' reminds him of how he ran when he was younger – Farrah in the 10,000 metres, Bolt in the 100 metres, Kemboi in the steeplechase. He muses as to whether it is too late for him to take up any new sports – kayak sprint, Taekwondo, boxing or the pommel horse. He asks a continual stream of unanswerable questions: why hasn't he heard of Greg Rutherford before now, why doesn't Mo Farrah's wife look happier, how could he get onto the Olympic Committee to hand out the medals?

The closing ceremony will see the end of Tea Taster's reign as the UK's most enthusiastic non-Olympian.

'I'm so glad it's all going well,' he says at the end of every day, eyes brimming with tears. 'l can't wait for Rio.'

I can.

Much love

Alison

# CHAPTER TWENTY-ONE

## A MAN WITH ONE LEG MADE ME CRY

**5 August 2012 – Special Yoga, London**

The things I'll do to keep busy. A Sunday morning at a transformational breathing workshop. It was held at Special Yoga. Seems a nice connection. The blurb told me it's a simple technique to open up the full potential of my breathing system for better physical and emotional well-being. I reckoned I could be quite good at it as I do have over 100% lung capacity. And I'm not a smoker.

It was weird! We breathed through cut-off water bottles and the woman next to me wailed and screamed. Even with all my angry emotions, I never felt like screaming. Perhaps I was doing it wrong? I am not sure what I was expecting but it was a disappointment. I hoped something miraculous would happen. All I got was a cut from the top of the bottle. And no sign of a FarwarParis anywhere. But it'll make for a good letter to Sabrine – she'll be impressed, although compared to her I'm a real amateur in the world of alternative therapies!

**8 August 2012 – Reiki Centre**

Reiki Ron has consulted with his psychic doctors and, in their wisdom, they believe my lesion will disappear today. Up until now, I have enjoyed my sessions but after that statement, I feel Ron is a fruit-loop.

But I do actually want to believe him.

I won't tell anyone of his prediction – well, maybe Alison; she'll understand.

## 10 August 2012 – Guildford Hospital

PET scan results are in.

No extra lesions. Just the original 7mm bastard. This is 'great' news and I can have key hole surgery to remove my unwanted companion.

I asked if a lesion is a tumour. Apparently it is but it's not yet known if mine is cancerous, although the chances are high. I will have 5% of the lung removed but as I'm over 100% lung capacity I reckon that will probably just take me down to 100%!

The consultant seemed very relaxed about it and said he'd operate in a couple of weeks when he's back from holiday. It was like we were discussing the removal of a wart.

I wanted to shout that this is my third round of cancer, that my chances of surviving are trickling away by the day and that I need him to take it more seriously. But of course, he is taking it seriously; it's just that he sees it every day.

## 12 August 2012

Olympic Closing Ceremony tonight. I cried but then that's all I've done for the last 3 weeks anyway. I don't want it to end. Along with the rest of the nation, and especially Tea Taster it seems, I've loved it.

**6 September 2012 – Olympic Stadium, London**

Buoyed up by Olympic enthusiasm, we got ourselves to the Paralympics tonight. We had brilliant seats, brilliant view, brilliant atmosphere and a Union Jack flag. Jonny Peacock won his 100m T44 final in style, claiming gold and a Paralympic record. I cried. Ruth cried. I hugged Neil. Neil hugged me. We all hugged each other, including the woman in the next seat.

**8 September 2012**

Called Danny to wish him a happy birthday. I didn't tell him about the cancer. It's his birthday, for goodness sake. Neil says I should have told him. I don't want to be responsible for how other people deal with my cancer but I feel I don't have a choice. Like I'm a curse. Bad news, Billy. I don't want to always be the damp squib but I am.

**13 September 2012 – London**

I think I enjoyed lunch today with Sabrine but I'm not sure as all I could taste were chilli flakes. She's lost most of her sense of taste through chemo and kindly assumed I had too as she sprinkled them liberally all over our vegan delights. Her bowel cancer has gone to her lung but they can't operate so she's back on the chemo poison. She was full of kind questions about my surgery but all I felt was guilt.

She asked if I used tahini. I had no idea what she was talking about. Was it a drug? She was shocked at my ignorance and insisted we call into Wholefoods on the way home. She promised it would change everything. Imagine my disappointment when I discovered it was just a form of peanut butter made with sesame.

She's thinking of suspending her treatment so she can visit a German clinic for some alternative therapies. She is far more adventurous than me; I thought the Hungarian dog medicine was cutting edge. She's gutsy, I'll give her that. Size of a sparrow but gutsy. Perhaps that's how you have to be when you'll be leaving a child behind?

## Who's Your Inspiration?

**15 Sept 2012**

Dear Brian

Save this letter for the hospital – well, I mean you don't have to, but I thought it might fill a few moments of post operation recovery time.

Over the last few weeks I've met a couple of women who've really inspired me, perhaps in the same way that Sabrine inspires you. I have to say, normally I wouldn't write about inspirational people because, let's be honest, no one likes an over-achiever. And one man's inspiration is another man's yawn. But having watched you over the last year or so, I'm beginning to take a different view on how we can improve our lives and what and who we should aspire to.

I'll start off with the elder woman, just to be respectful. I was at a school friend's wedding, sitting next to her Auntie June and Uncle Derek, a couple in their 70s. Uncle Derek was in a wheelchair, Auntie June a natty dresser but with teeth that hadn't seen a dentist for many years. As we chatted, I began to see why my friend is so fond of them. They were great company, making jokes with each other and bantering with the whole table. He would occasionally poke fun at her and she'd retaliate by telling him to shut up. She would then turn to me and say, 'He's a super chap, really, you know.'

She told me he'd been in the RAF and the Olympics, and went on to show me a couple of beautiful rings he'd designed and had made for her. I asked her how Uncle Derek had ended up in a wheelchair. She told me that when they met, he was a dashing officer in the RAF they'd married quickly, she giving up work in the hope of starting a family.

'We wanted a football team,' she joked. 'Well, I did.'

But on Derek's 23rd birthday, a motorbike accident put him in hospital with a broken spine. Discharged 15 months later, he was paralysed from the waist down, all June's dreams of a super-size family gone. Derek's Olympic triumphs were at the Paralympics and his creative design of rings was a skill he'd worked on over the years while sitting in his chair. But not for a minute did June think she was anything other than privileged to be married to Derek. Her big family was just something that wasn't meant to happen; instead, she was meant to spend all of her 55 years of married life caring for her 'super chap'.

But when I'd first met her, I thought she was just another old-aged pensioner. How wrong you can be!

Before the wedding, I spent a weekend in Wales. On route, I stopped off in Bristol to see my friend who I'd met in India. You may remember she was the one who I'd shared a room with, me telling her how fabulous my life is – charity auctions, art, going to Downing St... Not until the end of my time there did she happen to mention she'd founded and been running a charity for 16 years and had been awarded an honorary doctorate from Bristol University. Yes, she was far more fabulous than me – she just didn't go on about it.

I stopped off to meet her at her charity – a media centre: a cutting-edge building made from straw, she'd told me. But as I weaved my way around South Bristol council estates, I began to suspect that her straw centre was probably some shack in a field. What would a cutting-edge media centre be doing in this deprived area? Isn't media essentially all about the glamour? We'd soon see how fabulous she really was!

I turned a corner, passed a run-down parade of shops and there on my right was the Knowle West Media Centre - an imposing two-storey building with floor to ceiling glass frontage, car park and beautifully laid out gardens. Wow.

Inside, they were in the middle of presentations for an artist in residence programme. Some of the artists were already established, others emerging, some from UK, others from overseas. All felt the opportunity to work with this community was a prize worth competing for.

Later, I was shown around the centre. My friend had commissioned the building, the local community designed it, and then through her passion to bring art to this community, she peopled it with artists and teachers. Her latest triumph was a photography project for teenagers. Such was the success, one 18-year-old, post course, had cornered the local market in prom photography and had already earned enough money to put herself through university.

But when I'd first met my charity-champion friend, I thought she was just another public sector office worker - how wrong you can be!

Obviously inspired by these two women, and because everything works in threes, I decided to observe myself this week to see where I could make changes and become an inspiring woman.

My week has gone something like this:

At the doctor's for a woman's check-up, I mentioned that my recent kidney infection had left me with an embarrassingly weak bladder. The doctor diagnosed that the infection was perhaps still lingering. I was quite happy with this until I heard her utter the line, 'But if the test comes back clear, then we'll make an appointment for you to see the incontinence nurse.' Incontinence nurse! Surely, I'm about 30 years off needing the incontinence nurse! How inspiring can I be if I'm considered to be incontinent?

Needing a boost, I visited my sister. Being an auntie is an easy place to start on the journey of inspiring others.

As I was dressing one morning, my two-year-old niece walked into the bedroom. I was in my bra and knickers, rooting round in the wardrobe.

'Auntie Ali,' she called out, 'what are you wibbly wobbling for?'

I know she meant 'looking for' but it's 'wibbly wobbling' that came out her mouth when she looked at me. Inspirational people don't wibble wobble, do they, Bri?

So instead, I choose you to be my 3rd inspiration – yes, I know you're not a woman but just go with me on this.

Very quietly and humbly, you've learnt to live with cancer, facing each moment of adversity with the acceptance required and always finding the strength, humour and a way to be with others. So, maybe this is what I need to do – find the strength, humour and time for others, and someone out there may just be a little inspired by me in turn.

Much love, Bri

Alison

# CHAPTER TWENTY-TWO

## BUSMAN'S HOLIDAY

**17 September 2012 – John Radcliffe Hospital, Oxford**

Killing time in yet another waiting room of another hospital. My slot has been delayed by an emergency operation for some poor soul.

I am sporting my debonair dressing gown, which only gets an outing on these hospital visits. Neil is dressed more conventionally, reading the paper, although I can tell he's only skimming the words.

I don't tell him I'm again looking forward to the anaesthetic – the sensation of drifting away, losing control and surrendering to whatever happens. No thinking. No panic. I could be turning into one of those 'shock' stories on the front of the gossip magazines.

*Addicted To Surgery – Can't Stop, Won't Stop.*


**18 September 2012 – John Radcliffe Hospital, Oxford**

A pork chop! Had I really ordered that in my post-surgery fug? A great big, gristly thing on a bed of mash, swimming in gravy. Long gone are the days when a pork chop and onion gravy would have been a treat. The nurse took it away and came back with my cheese omelette and salad, saying the patient next door was equally disturbed as to what was on his plate.

They have removed all the drains except for the one coming from the lung. Am out of bed, walking up and down the ward, wheeling along the bag of bloody gunk coming out of the lung.

### 19 September 2012 – John Radcliffe Hospital, Oxford

I am constipated. No bowel movements since Monday. They say I can't go home until I've passed something, so I'm walking laps of the ward to encourage movement. Wonder if this is what Alison would imagine when she says I'm inspirational?

### 20 September 2012 – John Radcliffe Hospital, Oxford

Time in hospital is odd. This morning, all I had to worry about was a bit of constipation but by this afternoon we were in the tricky arena of a deflated lung. I'm warned that this is what may happen when they remove the drain. Lack of air and suffocating or choking, I'm imagining.

None of that actually happens and I'm told I'm all set to go home once I've pooed.

By 7pm, still no sign of a poo but I tell the nurse I've been so I'm off home tomorrow. I shall have no problem pooing on my own toilet seat. Over the last 2 years my bowels and I have got to know each other very well.

**22 September – 2012**

Bowels – and the earth – moved. Even Colin refuses to walk past the bathroom door.

**2 October 2012**

With my arms at my side, you can't see the scars. Two tiny holes. The nurse taking the stitches out told me I should be proud of my battle scars – they show I've survived. Why are the only people who say this those without scars?

**7 Oct 2012**

Hi Brian

At last, I get myself together and write a letter. This weekend I have laid low with a horrid cold. I knew working too much would lead to becoming run down. I haven't been ill since I finished working properly and this is a sure sign I've strayed from my path of a better-balanced life. And quite the opposite to you, it seems, with your speedy recovery. Practice makes perfect! I have become rather blasé about your illness and your operations. I now assume your recovery will always be quick, I assume that the cancer won't kill you and that we'll all live happily ever after.

Recently, I heard the quote: 'Never let the fear of dying get in the way of the joy of living.' It reminded me of a chap I worked with in my early twenties and still know today. He had a heart transplant at 20 and had recovered well but as he now approaches 40, he is facing a new challenge.

For the last 20 years he has eaten and drunk exactly what he's fancied, smoked like a chimney and taken not one jot of exercise. He's never bothered to pursue a career (although has always worked) and has pretty much led a life that suited him and only him.

He chose to live this way, believing he'd never make it to middle age. But now, with no sign of his transplanted heart ever giving out, it's starting to dawn on him that he may live for another 40 years. This realisation has stressed him to no end and he now has high blood pressure. He wants to be more healthy but 20 years of not letting the fear of dying get in the way of the joy of living has somewhat conditioned him to have a 'what the hell' attitude.

Ireland hit a new low this week. As you know, I have Siobhan and Connor on my team. Siobhan rarely does what's asked nor very much at all. Connor is brilliant but is only on my project part time. I've asked if I can lose Siobhan and have Connor full time instead.

The Board says I can't. We are now at the point where Siobhan's non-activity is jeopardising the project outcome. Yesterday, Donal, one of the board members, called me.

'Hello Alison,' he sang. Donal has a broad Derry accent and I have to concentrate hard to understand him. 'I think you're upset with Siobhan.'

'I am.'

'I have a question for you, Alison,' he continued. 'If Siobhan was to be... No, Alison, let me change my question. If I said to you, "Alison, you have to choose tomorrow if it's Siobhan or Connor who is hit by a bus", which one would you choose?'

Hit by a bus? Choose? Was I really having this conversation with a Board member of an international company? And death-by-bus was to be our criteria for whether someone should continue to work on my project?

I really do think this has to mark the end of my time in Ireland, Brian. If that's not the universe telling me something then I don't know what is.

Lots of love

Alison

# CHAPTER TWENTY-THREE

## WHAT'S OCCURRIN'?

**16 October 2012**

Sabrine's funeral tomorrow. I can't believe she's gone. Alison is coming with me. Says I shouldn't go alone. I'm sure I'll be fine.

**17 October 2012**

I wasn't fine. I sobbed. The kind of sobbing that's the reserve of close family. The kind of sobbing expected of a 9-year-old child. But my tears were not for Sabrine. My tears were for the guilt of still being alive. And how long before this is me?

**20 Oct 2012**

Hi Brian

Goodness what a week for you – you just got yourself out of hospital and then the tragedy of Sabrine's death. It was a truly beautiful funeral but seeing her son on the front pew made me weep. It was touching hearing Sabrine's sister thank you for the letters you'd sent, and her asking if they could keep them for her son's memory box.

Children seem to be a theme of my week. Tea Taster has a problem – Alfie. The graffiti and the weed are one thing, and of course, not ideal, but they don't potentially affect his future. What is more worrying is the latest threat to exclude him from school, and in his final GCSE year. Alfie is spirited, funny, and one day will be something very special but right now he's a complete pain in the arse, making the whole family's life a misery, bunking off school on an almost daily basis or, when he is there, bad-mouthing the teachers. I know Tea Taster wants me to be there more, to support him with all this but I'm not sure I'm the ideal person for the job. Am I?

It was while walking home the other day, having just spoken to Tea Taster on the phone about Alfie's latest escapade (stolen a dictionary from the local library so he can check his graffiti spelling and put the police off the scent) I bumped into the IT bloke I used to work with. You remember – I had him down as a closet gay when he rejected my advances, only to see him years later out and proud with his stunning South American girlfriend.

I did quite literally bump into him – on Chiswick High Road. He had an unsettling beaming smile across his face and greeted me with an unexpected chest-crunching hug. Six weeks ago, he'd become a father, he told me. I did the usual congratulatory shit but he mistook me for someone who would be interested in the details of his wife's labour - gushing about the pain, contractions, forceps, emergency caesarean... I feigned interest for a few moments and then made a move to leave but no, he had more to say.

'It's not too late for you,' he offered.

'I'm sorry?'

'Yes, you could have your own too, you know. It's not too late. There's things they can do now.'

I opened my mouth but nothing came out.

He continued: 'My friend's just had her first and she's 46. And my wife is 41.'

Finally, I spluttered, 'Oh, it's not for me thanks. I have lots of godchildren and a niece and nephew - that's enough.'

'But it's not like having your own. It's not too late. You should try it. Talk to your boyfriend.'

The truth is, Bri, I genuinely, genuinely have never wanted to be a mother. And still don't. Maternal feelings are as alien to me as a night of passion with a woman would be to you. But if that is true, why did I cry as I walked away?

Much love in my confusion

Alison

**22 October 2012**

I keep thinking about Alison's letter about the chap with the heart transplant and the phrase she mentioned, which I now can't get out of my head.

'Never let the fear of dying get in the way of the joy of living.'

Sabrine's funeral made me realise we're all in a queue, we just don't know how close we are to the front.

**4 November 2012**

Today I felt disorientated, daunted by the fragility and uncertainty of my life, and so I called Alison. A couple of years ago, I'd have never thought to look to her for wisdom and understanding. I barely knew her. But now she's my first port of call. She told me to read The Tibetan Book of Living & Dying, which she'd recently given me. I had been put off by the title but maybe now is the time to start. She also reminded me about Kris Carr's Crazy Sexy Cancer blog – she's never actually looked at it but she thought maybe I needed to revisit it.

## 5 November 2012

At Kris Carr's suggestion, I gave myself a 24-hour time limit on feeling fragile and now I feel better. Seems that Alison and Ms Carr know a thing or two about cancer.

## 9 November 2012 – Penny Brohn Cancer Care, Bristol

Penny Brohn have a cancellation and I've been offered the place. The timing couldn't be better.

Since discovering motorway services with The Bag, I've become quite partial to a coffee stop. In the queue, the man in front struck up a conversation. He was on his way to Barry Island for a conference and this naturally led on to jokes about Gavin and Stacey and my childhood visits to that part of Wales. He hovered around until I got my coffee and asked if I had to rush off.

Bit odd, but as I had time to spare, we sat outside Starbucks, inhaled diesel fumes and chatted. He was a nice enough guy: young, attractive and keen to share his less than extraordinary life story. Then he asked if I had to go to Bristol or would I consider driving on to Barry Island as he had a hotel room. I felt the draw, but only of flattery, so I thanked him for his kind offer but said I really did need to get to Bristol.

For the last 2 years, it has never occurred to me that I may still be attractive. But it has even less occurred to me that I may want a night of passion in Barry Island.

## 12 November 2012 – Penny Brohn Cancer Care, Bristol

As I left Penny Brohn, I resisted the urge to head west to Barry, and instead headed east. To home. To Neil and to Colin. I said goodbye to Penny Brohn – the building, the garden and the staff. And to Sabrine. Over the last 2 years they have taught me how to live with my cancer but I think this was my last visit.

## 15 November 2012

Letter arrived with date for appointment to get results of lesion biopsy. I'm not sure I will go.

## 17 November 2012

Neil asked why I had my new mantra:

*"Never Let the Fear of Dying Get in the Way of the Joy of Living"*

stuck up on the kitchen cupboard door if I'm going to be a scaredy-cat.

## 24 November 2012 – North Hampshire Hospital, Basingstoke

The lesion was cancerous. But it is out now. I will be back in 6 months' time for a scan and blood test. This is how life will now be. Time is limited.

## 25 November 2012

Until Alison began writing, I didn't know the pleasure of re-reading a letter. Today I went back to the Point & Purchase scheme at EuroDisney, Sticky Toffee Pudding-gate and holiday in Scarborough. Reading about the people in her life reminds me how precious people are in mine.

## 26 November 2012

Told Neil we need to get on with life, at least for the next half year (it seems longer when you say it like that). I'm organizing a murder mystery weekend with our closest friends for his 50th, a huge Christmas and a safari in the new year. There is no time to waste. If we have to live from one scan to the next, then let's do it in style.

Neil says this is fine but questions whether it is really necessary to have

*"Never Let the Fear of Dying Get in the Way of The Joy of Living"*

in a frame in every room. He says it's not the sentiment he objects to, more the font.

## 6 December 2012

Alison popped over so I could can help her with her tax return. I am flattered she trusts me with her financial details.

**7 Dec 2012**

Hi Brian

I did it. I pressed send. I did it. Thank you so much for sorting out all that tax return stuff. I do so hate all that.

Before I start on today's story, I want to take a moment to reflect on my visit to your house the other evening when you talked about Sabrine, the guilt of surviving and living from one scan to the next. People come into our lives for all sorts of reasons and it seems Sabrine has left you with something rather special. I noticed it as we chatted. A change. You seemed so calm, so accepting of your life and in charge of your own happiness. You seem to have a new energy – Neil isn't just having a birthday, you're throwing him a party; you're not just having a holiday, you're going on an adventure; and you're not just having a Christmas pudding, you're having a Heston Blumenthal Hidden Sauce Figgy Pudding from Waitrose! Once we accept our life and decide to enjoy it, we become grateful for what it can be. And then we feel empowered. And then change and hope become possible. When someone touches our life in such a way, we are given a true gift.

Today's story is Helen's. I went to school with Helen. She left at 16 as she was mad about horses and wanted to work at a stables. Her life continued in quite a predictable way: she married at 21 and had two kids. Her kids are now grown up, one working, the other at university. Her husband ran off with a younger woman several years ago and Helen has since filled her life with a boyfriend, three horses, a full-time job and lots of friends. I meet up with her once a month, and having known her for such a long time, thought I knew everything about her.

Last week, while out celebrating her birthday, she mentioned she'd been to Paul's funeral that morning and how sad it was. One of the girls at the table asked who Paul was, and for the first time, I heard Paul and Helen's story.

Years ago, Helen managed a shelter for the homeless and even with all of her northern pragmatism, she was at times extremely tested. She saw the worst of what homelessness offers: being threatened at knife and gun point by drug addicts, alcoholics dying in the night too drunk to find shelter and teenagers abused by parents they almost dare to trust and then running away again.

Paul was a regular visitor to the shelter. Social Services classed him as 'capable', but while he could function in some ways, he couldn't hold down a job, interact with strangers, keep himself warm nor cook. In many ways Paul was incapable, but without being classed as such, Social Services would not take responsibility.

Helen described Paul as a wonderful character with great charisma and wit. He was an alcoholic and had spent much of his life in and out of hospital. It was always Helen he contacted when he was admitted and again when he was discharged, usually having discharged himself. Helen battled many times with Social Services to find Paul housing, but each time she was successful, within a few months, Paul would abandon his house and return to the streets. The only constant in his life was Helen.

Four years ago, Helen moved jobs but continued to keep in contact with him. She took care of his money, bought and cooked food for him when she knew where he was, and never gave up her struggle to have him certified as 'incapable' so he could receive proper care.

Last year Paul contracted a terminal illness. With great lucidity, which at other times eluded him, he chose not to have treatment. Helen continued to care for him as best she could, visiting him weekly in the council house she'd managed to secure. The house was furnished with one mattress but Paul refused to put money in the meter for gas or electricity so he lived in the freezing cold, often lying in wet clothes from walks he'd taken in the pouring rain.

Last week, at the age of 58, Paul died. Helen wanted to organise the funeral but as she wasn't next-of-kin so she wasn't allowed – Social Services would take care of all that, she was told. She asked if she could have his possessions, (a hat and a radio), but was told no – Social Services would be dealing with those. He left £4000 in a bank account, which the state took as he left no will.

So that morning, on her birthday, Helen attended Paul's welfare-organised funeral.

She was the only person there.

So why had I never heard of Paul?

Because looking after Paul was just something Helen did; she didn't need us all to know nor wanted our praise. Helen showed Paul what no one else ever had – real friendship and love.

'He was so lucky to have you in his life,' I said to her as she concluded her story.

'No,' she replied. 'I was lucky to have him in mine. He was a gift of a friend.'

Our connections come in the most unusual forms, don't they, but the best ones make our lives immeasurably better.

Much love

Alison

# CHAPTER TWENTY-FOUR

## THE RESULTS ARE IN

**10 December 2012**

I haven't told anyone, other than Neil, about my new attitude to life and living it to love it rather than to exist, but it seems Alison has noticed. And she's right, I do want us to celebrate birthdays, have adventures, eat fabulous food.

Although I guess the many framed Comic Sans mantras may have been a giveaway!

**16 December 2012 – Bath**

Will Neil's 50th birthday celebrations never end? Although I only have myself to blame as I arranged them. A house party with a murder mystery evening with our 12 closest friends. I felt rather dapper in my charity-shop-purchased morning suit for my role as 'Jeeves, the Butler'. Neil is in full deerstalker, tweeds and pipe for his character – Sherlock Holmes. Gillian is the glamorous Lady Penelope, Alison is a real plain Jane as Glenda the penniless librarian (totally out of character), and Tea Taster is totally in character as 'a posh man from the country'.

As we got more drunk and rowdy we all slipped out of character, except Alison.

Of course, she had the stamina to stay with the game as everyone else lost interest. She won the whole thing, including the Oscar for best actor.

I haven't laughed so much in ages.

Today is a bit of a write-off, exactly as it should be.


**18 December 2012**

Buttoned my shirt up the wrong way this morning. The woman pushing the wheelchair, right at the beginning of my treatment – I wonder if her cardigan ever got buttoned up the right way. And were her sacrifices worth it? I want to ask Neil that question but I don't dare. All I can know is that I don't want to ever be without my cardigan.


**19 December 2012**

Three things to do today:

1. Make a donation to Penny Brohn in memory of Sabrine
2. Book the safari
3. Sort out super-size Xmas, getting balance right between not scaring people into thinking it's my last and enjoying it whether it is or not.

**31 December 2012**

Christmas has been exhausting – just as I wanted it to be. So, tonight, it'll be a quiet one.

What a year! We survived it. I survived it. New Year's resolution – survive another.

**5 Jan 2013**

Hi Brian

Happy New Year.

Have you ever heard of Albert Hammond? I was reminded of him this week as a Whitney Houston song played on the radio and the presenter mentioned something about the prolific song writer who had penned it. I remembered a friend telling me she was going to an Albert Hammond concert a few years ago. Not knowing anything about him, I had googled him at the time to discover he'd not only written Whitney Houston's 'One Moment in Time' but also Starship's 'Nothing's Gonna Stop Us Now' and

Julio Iglesias's 'To All the Girls I've Loved Before'. He is credited on hundreds of millions of record sales.

But the thing I most remember is that she was seeing him in a local, small venue. The man who had written some of the most famous songs in pop history and made stars into mega-stars, putting them into arenas and stadiums, was gigging in your average, everyday concert venue! No arenas and stadiums for Albert. But he must have made a fortune from his song-writing. Surely, he doesn't need to gig at all.

Of course, he doesn't but it's his passion – writing, singing, performing. He doesn't care how others perceive him; he's doing what he enjoys. He's following his passion.

This has got me to thinking. (And what with it being a new year and everything...) All this consultancy work has been great (well, has provided some good content for letters) but I feel I'm back on the corporate treadmill. I have slipped back into everything I wanted to escape. And so I thought what would Brian do?

I have an idea – I'm going to do a creative writing MA. I know not just anyone with a pencil case can rock up and do an MA, and I don't know if my writing is good enough – I have only ever written letters to you, Bri, and that's probably not enough – but if I don't try, I'll never know so I'm going to give it a go.

Last week, I called in at the Special Yoga centre to see Jo and some of the children. Being back there reminded me how I'd been when I first left work and got involved with their art auction. I had no idea what I was doing but I was learning, I was being challenged, and I was giving it a go. That description sounds more like you than me these days. And as Jo so often says, 'the angels will always look after us.'

Speaking of angels, I found something today that brought a tear and a smile.

I'd left a bag at Tea Taster's some time ago and only retrieved it this last weekend. When I emptied it out, I found an envelope addressed to 'Ali'. Inside was a scrap of crumpled paper.

*Ali*

*I know you like letters 'cos you rite them to that man.*

*Sorry about polis today. Polis are bolox but you realy helped.*

*Thanx*

*Alf*

I asked Tea Taster if he'd suggested to Alfie he write a note but he knew nothing about it.

Of course, now I feel guilty for cursing Alfie at the time, for feeling so hard done by myself. He is, after all, no different to the rest of us, just trying to find his way in the world. Me, Albert and Alfie!

Much love

Alison

### 8 January 2013

New Year begins, with highs and lows, but this time not about me. One neighbour had a baby. Other neighbour died.

I have a New Year resolution (along with surviving another year) – sort out Alison. Is she actually going to get married I wonder? Men like Tea Taster don't come along often, and certainly not often enough for Alison to pass him by. Wonder if I should subtly ask in an email? Or maybe invite her round for lunch – just me and her. Don't want to seem nosy but I feel an intervention is needed. Perhaps it's finally my turn to help her.

### 14 January 2013 – Safari

Being on safari is exhausting. Up at 4.30am and on the drive by 5.00am. But my God, is it worth it.

Ever since I was a boy, I have wanted to see a leopard and today, there one was. Mesmerisingly graceful. Strong.

I decided not to spoil the mood by mentioning the leopard sighting had ticked something off my bucket list. Neil doesn't like mention of my bucket list.

### 16 January 2013 – Safari

Today we were blessed with a pride of 10 lions lazing in the sun. I had an inexplicably strong urge to climb out of the Jeep, walk over to them and sit down. I wanted to be part of their calm presence. Fortunately, I resisted the urge. Although what a way to go – providing sustenance to nature.

### 18 January 2013 – Safari

Last day on the reserve. I gave my safari clothes to our driver. I was going to give them to a charity but he said he has an uncle and aunt who are both my size. I didn't question further.

### 6 February 2013 – North Hampshire Hospital, Basingstoke

Only Neil knows today is the day. Scan day. I take Alison with me. In letter form – my distraction and comfort.

### 7 February 2013

Ban scan-talk

**8 February 2013**

Walked Colin


**9 February 2013**

Walked Colin


**10 February 2013**

Feel I should respond to Alison's last letter, tell her that the creative writing course is an excellent idea, that you'd have to have 2 glass eyes not to see writing has become her passion, but I can't. I want to be happy for her but not today. Scanxiety makes you selfish, isolated, less human.


**11 February 2013**

Colin was too exhausted to walk today. As was I. Denial is very tiring. Instead, I watched back-to-back episodes of Sex in the City. I wonder which character Alison might be? She has traits of them all, even Charlotte, as we mustn't forget her experience in the art world. And she was a lawyer like Miranda. I think she'd like to think she was Samantha. But soon, she'll be totally Carrie as a writer, finally having found her Mr Big. I text her to tell her she definitely should apply for the MA.

**12 February 2013**

The neighbours must think I'm in training for The Great British Bake-Off. We can't eat all the cupcakes I'm baking so they're getting a daily delivery. You have to be so precise with baking. It's like a meditation. No wonder Mary Berry looks so well.

**13 February 2013**

Where's a distracting letter from Alison when you need one?

**15 February 2013**

Still no scan news. No news must be good news? But then what? I have no plan for the rest of my life. Retire? Find a job? Who wants to employ a 55-year-old man with hovering cancer? At least with actual cancer I had a purpose. God, did I really write that?

**18 February 2013**

The results are in.

No Evidence of Disease.

**19 February 2013**

Still hasn't sunk in that it is now wholly possible the fucker has actually fucked off.

**20 February 2013**

I still can't believe it. Neil and I hugged again this morning. And cried. Again. And hugged again. It's too big to deal with. And I hardly dare to be excited but, at least for the next 6 months, till the next scan, I can crack on with whatever there is to crack on with. Sent Alison a text with the good news. She replied that my news had made her cry. As I hadn't told anyone I was going for the scan, I don't know what to do about telling everyone else. Think I will just leave it at Alison, and Gillian, of course.

# OMG

**21 Feb 2013**

Dear Brian

While we have celebrated your amazing news on the phone, text and email, I think it only fitting I mark the occasion with a letter. I hope the headed paper says everything about how happy I am for you. I can't start to imagine how you're feeling but it must involve a lot of smiling, as well as a fair dollop of incredulity.

Now, that's enough about you. Back to me. I'm stuck in the hell of my MA application. It is all very well you saying an MA is a great idea

but you don't have to write a 5,000 word story.
How do you write 5,000 words? My letters aren't
even 1,000.

And what shall I write about? Forget planning
your future life, Bri, I need you on story
planning.

Much love

Alison

**22 February 2013**

Changed my mind – told everyone. They have seen me through the
bad scans so they need to be a part of the good one too. Seems it has
brightened up a lot of people's day, judging by the responses to my
texts. I can't quite believe Alison shed a tear. I wonder if this is the
end of the letters. I'll miss them, but now we meet and talk regularly
like best friends, so perhaps we don't need them?

**25 February 2013**

It is like I have won the lottery but have no idea what to spend the
money on. The safari was my holiday of a lifetime. I have Colin and
Neil. My friends and family. This is why I had surgery after surgery, so
I could live the life I am already living. But what do I do when everyone
is at work and I can no longer say my full-time job is getting well?

**5 March 2013 – Reiki Centre**

Reiki today but no Ron – he's been 'let go'. No explanation. I have a new healer but something is missing. Time to move on.

**9 March 2013**

Still no word on the Hitchcock wedding. It is time for an intervention.

# CHAPTER TWENTY-FIVE

## TIME FOR THAT NEW JOURNAL

**9 March 2013**

Dear Alison

What can I say? It's time for me to send a letter to you. Your letters have meant everything to me.

They have been my companion in the chemo ward (even helped me make some friends), connected me back to a world I felt so distanced from (even though your world is a bit crazy at times) and, most importantly, made me laugh time and time again.

It's like you've been there with me the whole time.

Nothing prepares you for the isolation and loneliness of cancer – all those friends you hope will step up but don't; the hours you spend alone while everyone else goes to work or the pub.

And then the worst bit of all – the isolation you impose on yourself as you can't bear another conversation about it with a neighbour, another relative to comment how lucky you are not to have lost your hair, another person to pity you.

But through all of that I have had your letters – my letterbox friends. You have shared your world with me and taken me away from my own.

Your presence has been constant, gentle and unobtrusive.

Getting to know about the people in your life has reminded me so often how precious those are in mine; that those connections are what make our lives worth living; that all the surgeries and radio and chemotherapies are worthwhile if it means we can spend just a little more time with the ones we love; that our lives shine brighter when we share them with our precious people.

I believe Ben, Scarlett, Alfie and Billy (and even growling Lizzie) are precious to you, that your life with them is what you've been looking for and what the last two crazy years have been leading to. Am I right?

If I am right, then I have to ask, when's the wedding?

You take care

Brian

**17 March 2013**

Dear Brian

I don't intend for the whole of this letter to have a serious tone but I am starting with one. Thank you for your kind (and very unexpected) letter. I only ever wanted my letters to cheer you up through your treatment. I never expected they would do more. I'm so pleased they have impacted your life as much as they have mine. However, I also know that really your letter is asking the question everyone's wondering: why isn't she getting on and planning a wedding? Does she even really want to get married?

The answer is yes - I do. Tea Taster is definitely the one for me; I know that beyond any doubt, regardless of how different we are. He's kind, loyal and trusting but, above all, he makes me laugh (both at and with him) and, while it's taken me a long time to learn how important these qualities are, I finally get it.

But you are quite right; I have been procrastinating - well, more like ostrich-heading. Even Tea Taster's patience is being tested. But none of this is about him; it's about me and, more specifically, me becoming a step-mum. Not because I don't want to - Alfie, Billy and Scarlett are great kids - but because I know I will be a very poor version of a mother, step or otherwise. I can't cook, I don't know anything about teenage hormones and the fascination of the X-Box and Minecraft is beyond me. I know I can learn but what if I'm really not made for it, in the same way Cruella De Vil isn't made for dog-sitting? I feel as if I'm back to the panic attack days of the charity art auction when I vowed not to venture out of my comfort zone again. I've told Tea Taster and he says none of it matters, that the Hitchcocks are a better family with me than without me and he is a better man because of that. But he also says it's fine if I don't want to join Family Hitchcock, if I don't want to marry him, be with him – he knows, as my mum has always warned, it's a lot to take on.

In your letter, you said that watching my life made you realise the value of your own and the people in it; the connections we make are what give our lives shape and meaning. At the same time, I have watched your life, seen you overcome every obstacle cancer has presented, even when the prognosis was at its most bleak; I have watched you grasp life with a passion and joy, be able to be vulnerable, and at many times be pushed so far outside your comfort zone, it's gone way beyond those suggested five pebbles. And you have done it all with such a gentle grace and style.

Often in these letters I have written about mothers – mothers with lovers, mothers with brats, my own mother. Each one of them is different; each one has made it up as they've gone along but they've all done the best job they possibly could. And they've all been guided by love.

So, if they can deal with the unknown, and you can, then perhaps I can too? It will be scary; it will be outside my comfort zone and sometimes I will crave a different life but I'm going to do it. So, we will have the best wedding with the best party and everyone will love it (or at least get very drunk). And I shall be the best step-mum I possibly can be. And if I'm not, at least I'll have some content for more letters.

There are, however, another couple of reasons to get on and plan a wedding: one is my mum and the other is you. Let me explain.

In a bid to keep my mum active through the winter and help with her wibbly wobbly legs illness, my sister and I persuaded her to get a treadmill. She rented one but quickly sent it back, claiming it made no difference to her leg strength and was a waste of her time and money. That was until she mentioned it to her rheumatology consultant, who said a treadmill was a wonderful idea, and within a week my mum had rented it back.

One day, while steadily exercising at her usual two miles an hour, and for reasons unknown, she decided to press the speed button. But not just once. Oh no, she pressed it so many times, the treadmill raced up to 12 mph, and my mum was catapulted off the back.

On the floor, her wrist trapped underneath the machine, belt still racing, she tugged and tugged till she managed to release her arm, breaking her watch in the process. By this time, of course, the sleeve of her jumper was chewed to nothing and her silk scarf had been sucked into the machine. Yes, you did read right: my mum wears a silk scarf while exercising. Nothing could save the scarf; it was shredded along with her confidence.

On hearing the news, Ben (I feel I should use his real name, now we are definitely to be hitched) commented that at those sorts of speeds she'd have swept the board at the Paralympics. But she refuses to get back on the 'damned machine', so needs something else to occupy her time, so I thought a daughter's wedding might fill the gap.

And then there's you, Bri. With life 'back to normal' and waiting for your next scan, I thought you could do with a project, and what better than to plan my wedding? Natasha has had the idea of a teepee on my sister's lawn, and as I've come to learn, Natasha always knows best. So how are you fixed for some research into teepee hire and decoration? And there'll be lots of other things to organise, I'm sure. Oh, Brian, you are going to be so busy. You will help, won't you? I'm not sure I can do it without you.

Much love

Alison

**21 March 2013**

Well, that's my next few months sorted — organizing Alison's wedding. She says she definitely wants to get married, so let's make it a wedding to remember. My chance to do something for her.

**24 March 2013 – Richmond Park.**

I met Alison for a walk in Richmond Park. We haven't been here together since the colostomy bag dilemma. We're true friends now, both of us in very different places.

I talked about Hungarian dog medicine and whether I should continue to take it. Alison chatted about her MA application and not being able to imagine writing the required 5,000 words. I told her to crack on and get it done and she told me to carry on with the moon-howling juice. And then we moved on to the main event – the wedding. It's going to be in a teepee in her sister's garden in Lincolnshire. I am tasked with sourcing a hog roast and Ottolenghi-style salads (which, in Lincolnshire, could just turn out to be coleslaw). She has titled me Head of Catering. I have a new purpose. I am not, however, Head of Bridal Dress. That's Natasha.

**28 March 2013**

Email from Alison. She's written a 5,000 word piece of fiction for her MA application and wants my critique. I am asked to comment on:

- Is it something that holds my interest?
- What works well?
- Is it grammatically correct?
- Do any words, sentences or paragraphs jar?
- Do I get a feel for the characters and place?

At first, I wondered how I could do this but, actually I do know her writing after 3 years, so I'm quite looking forward to being teacher. I have red pen at the ready.

**10 April 2013**

It's all about Alison these days! She's put me down as a referee for her MA applications. She's obviously taking this creative writing thing very seriously. Seems she really has found her passion. I wonder if this makes me her muse? But I guess that was only for the letters. Her new writing will be inspired by others. I will have to share her. Very honoured she chose me as referee.

**23 April 2013**

Well, I wasn't expecting this.

*Hi*
*For my hen night, I just want my closest chums, so no more than*
*seven of us.*

*Obviously, I want you to be there and I hope you will come. Dates to follow.*

I have never been on a hen night. Will there be a stripper? Will we have to wear a special T-shirt or sash? Doesn't sound much like Alison. I wonder who is Head of Hen Night?

## 26 April 2013

Well, that was quick. The hen night is booked. Still can't believe I'm invited. Natasha is in charge.

We've been asked to vote from these suggestions:

1) Karaoke (they wouldn't be suggesting that if they'd heard Alison sing)
2) Fire breathing workshop
3) Live sex show in Amsterdam (Oh God, really?)
4) Nude life drawing
5) Axe throwing and afternoon tea

My vote goes to an afternoon of nude life drawing.

## 27 April 2013

I have a pain in my throat and chest. Is this the cancer coming back? Every twinge, every pain rings cancer in my ears.

**28 April 2013**

I have a cold – a wonderful, snotty, rasping throat cold. No cancer but just a common, marvellous cold.

Feeling brave, I Google survival rates for Stage IV bowel cancer. I've never dared to before. 1 in 10 people will survive more than 5 years, it says.

I am starting to believe that, for the first time in my life, when it actually really matters, I could finally be in the 10% club.

**30 April 2013**

Dear Brian

I'm in the middle of canape-gate.

My mum offered to organise the canapes for the wedding as she knows a man who can get them cheap. I requested the canapes be vegetarian so everyone could eat them.

'Vegetarian?' my mum spluttered down the phone. 'How many of those have you got coming?'

Before I could answer she carried on.

'And what about children? How many of those are coming?'

'Not many. Why?'

'Well, we don't want them eating the canapes, do we?'

Good Lord no, as if it's not bad enough we've got vegetarians coming, there's now a chance we may have canape-eating toddlers too.

'If you want vegetarian canapes,' she said, 'then it's over to you. Goodbye.' And she put the phone down.

As I pondered the canape outburst, I recalled her incredulity on discovering my brother-in-law was a vegetarian.

Mum: 'Pete, you'll have some chicken, won't you?'

Pete: 'No, Olive. I'm a vegetarian'

Mum: 'What? Not even a bit of chicken?'

Pete: 'No, Olive, I don't eat meat or fish or wear leather'

Mum: (whispering to my sister) 'Pete can have a bit of chicken, can't he?'

Jane: 'No, he's a vegetarian'

Mum: 'But it's only a bit of chicken'

Jane: 'He'll not eat it'

Pete is handed a plate of vegetables with a knob of cheese on the side.

Pete: 'Olive, what's this?'

Mum: 'What Pete? The gravy?'

Pete: 'But, Olive, I'm a vegetarian'

Mum: 'I know. That's why you've got cheese. But you can eat gravy. It's lovely, Pete. Made with the chicken juices. It'll give your vegetables some flavour.'

So, Brian, can I put you in charge of canapes please? Oh, and while we're on with catering, Ben and I don't want a cake but we know everyone likes a cupcake. And you make a nice cupcake. Don't suppose you could rustle up 120 for the big day, could you? Remember, you are Head of Catering.

And now onto my very exciting news. You'll never guess what. I've had not one but two offers. For MAs. I can't believe it. I can write. Or I at least have the makings of a writer. I'm so excited. I haven't been this excited since I came second in my school's talent competition dressed as one quarter of ABBA singing 'Dancing Queen'. I shall start in October. It will be part time so I'll be able to continue with some work, just to keep the wolves from the door and pay for the wedding, but I shall have lots of time to write. Thank you so much for encouraging me to get on with my application. I did it. I did it. I did it. And all because of you. And the letters. And cancer.

When I started this letter, and with my MA news fresh in my mind, I thought about the first letter I sent you. Do you remember it? The first thing I told you about was my iron deficiency and I made big promises about comedy-headed notepaper. Little did we know then about the coming operations, chemotherapy, alkaline food, Hungarian dog medicine, healing, wedding, MA, all-clear and Colin. My promise was to cheer you up while you were going through your cancer journey. But now you are at the end. So, no need for any more letters.

Or then again, maybe I could amend my original offer. How about if I'd said I'd write letters to cheer you up while you're going through your cancer treatments and thereafter till you get the five years all-clear?

So, I think this means more letters to my wonderful friend.

Much love

Alison

# EPILOGUE

**June 17, 2022**

Dear Alison

Today is my 65th birthday. Yes 65! Let's just pause for a minute to take that in.

Since 2013 every one of my scans has shown No Evidence of Disease. If I spend time thinking about this, I become overwhelmed (and cry – getting rid of cancer hasn't seemed to get rid of the crying).

At 5 years, a consultant congratulated me for being in the 10% Survivors Club. Seems even now I'm still a fully paid-up member. How lucky am I?

In 2015 you graduated from Birkbeck University with a Creative Writing MA (and I graduated from having to read your endless drafts of short stories and come up with suitably encouraging responses to the question: 'Do you think it's any good?') What I do know as 'good' is you as a step-mum; you've bonded so easily with Ben's three children (and with far greater success than you ever bonded with Lizzie the Jack Russell).

Since 2013, your letters may have been less frequent but you're still encouraging me to go outside my comfort zone. Who else but you could have persuaded me, in 2016, to appear on the BBC's Listening Project, to talk about letters, friendship and the importance of connecting?

I don't think either of us imagined the next thing we'd do would be to set up our charity, From Me to You, but we both passionately felt we had found a way to tackle the isolation and loneliness which is so often experienced by someone living with cancer; helping people connect at a time when it's so much easier not to.

These days it's the charity fundraising which pushes me out of my comfort zone. It started with a 125km walk along the Camino de Santiago followed, 3 days later, by the London to Brighton Bike Ride (and you know how much I hate cycling!). And then, on the eve of my 62nd birthday, I did my first ever triathlon, which involved open water swimming in the Thames.

To my delight (and the irritation of my sporty friends) I was featured on the BBC Sport's website - for someone who was never in the 10%

Sporty Club this was a major win. My comedy-headed note paper today is taken from the website photo; it never fails to make me smile. And I haven't let you get away with sitting in your comfort zone either. I couldn't believe it when you told me that if I completed the triathlon you would busk in Carnaby Street to fundraise, being made all the more remarkable by the fact that we all know you were born without the singing gene.

I watched in amazement, shaking a collection tin, as people donated money (not sure if my amazement was that you were busking or that people were giving money!).

But the thing I think we're both most proud of is that every year our charity's Donate A Letter programme delivers thousands of letters from anonymous writers to those living with cancer in hospitals, hospices and at home.

Even before the Covid-19 pandemic there was much academic research into the effects of isolation and loneliness on our health (its impact being compared to obesity, smoking and physical inactivity) but then came the lockdowns and suddenly we all had first-hand experience of isolation and understood why we need to connect and communicate.

I kept all your letters, you know? Still have them in a box, still read them, still smile at the ridiculousness of your stories. They're a bit tatty now from being picked up, re-read and shared with others. Of course, every text, email and phone message I received from loved ones back then was equally appreciated but they're long deleted, each one only read or listened to once. But like the letters, they kept me connected and I will be forever grateful for the time and love that each and every one of those people gave me.

I am looking forward to seeing you later at my party. You'll know most people there and they you. New friends still ask what made you make that initial offer to write.

I tell them what you once shared with me that you felt sorry to hear my news and wanted to help but didn't want to get too involved; wanted to be able to keep your distance. I remember joking with you that your plan hadn't really worked out very well. You laughed, and then you said, and I can remember it word for word, it was the best mistake you'd ever made.

I wish everyone could have a friendship like ours, but I do believe that the most special friends turn up when you least expect them but most need them.

So, I hope you have your dancing shoes ready because tonight we're having a one hell of a party. We'll eat, we'll drink and we'll dance but most of all, we'll celebrate friendship, love and hope.

# FROM ME, TO YOU

Love

Brian xxx

# HOW TO WRITE A LETTER TO A FRIEND OR RELATIVE LIVING WITH CANCER

- Spoil your friend; a letter is like a hand-made gift. Choose some beautiful stationery.
- You'll need their address – we often don't have addresses anymore so you may need to ask.
- Don't be daunted – write a short note or postcard first saying that you've heard the news, you're thinking of them and you will write a letter soon.
- Collect stories, quotes, witty anecdotes, poems. All these things can fill your letters. If you can make your friend smile and feel connected with your world, they will feel less isolated in their own.
- Let the gossip flow – keep them in touch with life at work or social gossip, giving them a link to the real world. You could even start a humorous day-to-day journal of what's been happening in the office and include it in your letters.

- Don't feel guilty that you're having fun – tell your friend about films you've seen, concerts you've been to, books you've read. They want to hear about normal lives.
- Write from the heart – no matter how clumsy the words, if it's from the heart you can't go wrong.
- Get your letter to the post box – whether it's handwritten or typed, as long as it makes its way into an envelope and into the post, you've done a wonderful thing.
- Some people want to be private about their diagnosis – it's important to respect this.

# FURTHER READING AND USEFUL ADDRESSES

## ORGANISATIONS AND HELPLINES

**BOWEL CANCER UK**

UK's leading bowel cancer charity with a vision to create a future where no one dies of the disease.

Website: www.bowelcanceruk.org.uk
Telephone: 020-7940 1760
Email: admin@bowelcanceruk.org.uk

**CANCER RESEARCH UK**

Providing cancer information to the public, this charity works towards a day when all cancers are cured.

Website: www.cancerresearchuk.org

**COLOSTOMY UK**

A charity supporting and empowering people living with a stoma.

Website: www.colostomyuk.org
Telephone: 0800 328 4257
Email: hello@colostomyuk.org

**FROM ME TO YOU**

Working to alleviate the isolation and loneliness experienced by those living with cancer.

Website: www.frommetoyouletters.co.uk
Email: info@frommetoyouletters.co.uk

**MACMILLAN**

Helping everyone with cancer to live life as fully as they can.

Website: www.macmillan.org.uk
Telephone: 0808 808 00 00

**PENNY BROHN UK**

Helping those living with cancer to find ways to care for mind, body, emotions, spirit, heart and soul.

Website: www.pennybrohn.org.uk
Telephone: 0303 3000 118
Email: info@pennybrohn.org.uk

## BOOKS, BLOGS AND ARTICLES

- Anti-Cancer – A New Way of Life by Dr David Servan-Schrieber
- Crazy Sexy Diet by Kris Carr
  www.kriscarr.com
- Everyday Osho – 365 Meditations for the Here and Now by Osho
- Forks Over Knives by Del Soufre
  www.forksoverknives.com
- Kiss or Kill: Confessions of a Serial Climber by Mark Twight
- Ted Talks – Brene Brown – The Power of Vulnerability
- The Tibetan Book of Living and Dying by Sogyal Rinpoche
- Topic of Cancer by Christopher Hitchens in Vanity Fair August 2010

For more help and letter writing inspiration, please visit us at:
www.frommetoyouletters.co.uk

# ACKNOWLEDGMENTS

Writing a book can take a long time, and when it's you and a best friend scribbling away together, it can just be an excuse to spend more time together. It is the guidance and support of the people along the way which turn your jottings and musings into something to be proud of. We have so many people to thank for making this book a reality.

To our agent, Caroline Montgomery of Rupert Crew - none of this would have happened without your deep understanding of what we wanted to achieve, and your never-fading support. If this book has an absolute champion, it is you.

To Sumaira Wilson and Nikki East at our publishers, SpellBound - thank you for being touched by our story, and wanting to give it life.

To Emily Jeffery at BBC Radio Sussex - you were the catalyst for both this book and our charity. Your enthusiasm for our story of letters, friendship and hope inspired us to share it further.

To Nikki at Spellbound and Annette Steiner for creating a book cover which makes us smile every time we look at it.

To Luke Melia, who showed us how to tease out the true story in a true story, and for your enthusiasm and commitment to writing a screenplay which, one day, will share our story far and wide.

To Sue Lascelles and Emily Yau, for editing our early drafts with such constructive encouragement, empathy, and support. You gave us the confidence to reach the final draft.

To Julia Bell at Birkbeck University, Cathy Galvin at The Word Factory and Alexander Masters at Arvon, for instilling in us a love of words and teaching that stories change lives.

To the wondrous group of writing friends who read, steered, edited and buoyed us up right from the very start.

And finally, to our partners, Neil and Ben - one for always being there and the other for making great content for letters.

# PHOTO ATTRIBUTIONS

Chapter 1, July 18, 2010 - Photo by Pixabay on Pexels

Chapter 5, October 20, 2010 - Six weather Icons, by Sihan Liu

Chapter 7, November 21, 2010 - Photo by Rachel Claire on Pexels

Chapter 7, November 28, 2010 - Photo by Pixabay on Pexels

Chapter 7, December 07, 2010 - Photo by Karolina Grabowska on Pexels

Chapter 8, December 30, 2010 - Photo by Edward Howell on Unsplash

Chapter 10, March 05, 2011 - Six weather Icons, by Sihan Liu

Chapter 11, March 31, 2011 - Photo by Gasper Uhas on Unsplash

Chapter 12, May 03 2011 - Photo by Giancarlo Duarte on Unsplash

Chapter 15, September 24, 2011 - Photo by Chaitanya Pillala on Unsplash

Chapter 16, January 01, 2012 - Photo by Marina Hannah on Unsplash

Chapter 16, January 11, 2012 - Photo by Karolina Grabowska on @ Pexels

Chapter 17, January 24, 2012 - Photo by Pixabay on Pexels

Chapter 18, March 24, 2012 - Photo by Ricardo Esquivel on Pexels

Chapter 18, April 03, 2012 - Photo by Ekaterina Belinskaya on Pexels

Chapter 19, June 03, 2012 - Photo by Alexas_Fotos on Pixabay

Chapter 19, July 07, 2012 - Photo by Justin Smith on Pexels

Chapter 20, July 17, 2012 - Photo by StockSnap on Pixabay

Chapter 22, October 07, 2012 - Photo by Fahad Bin Kamal Anik on Unsplash

Chapter 23, December 07, 2012 - Photo by Nik on Unsplash

Chapter 24, January 05, 2013 - Photo by Suzy Hazelwood on Pexels

How to write a Letter - Photo by Krisztina Papp on Unsplash

# ABOUT THE AUTHORS

Alison Hitchcock's love of letter writing led her to an MA in Creative Writing, short stories published and a first novel (still languishing in a drawer!). She lives with husband Ben.

Brian Greenley is the award-winning co-founder of the charity From Me to You. He lives in Berkshire with partner Neil and constant companion Colin the dog.

Ingram Content Group UK Ltd.
Milton Keynes UK
UKHW022238040523
421244UK00004B/234